A History and Guide
to
Old Fort Niagara

• REVISED EDITION •

by
Brian Leigh Dunnigan

A History and Guide to Old Fort Niagara

by *Brian Leigh Dunnigan*

2007 Revised and Expanded Edition

OLD FORT NIAGARA ASSOCIATION, INC.
Old Fort Niagara National Historic Landmark
Fort Niagara State Park
Youngstown, New York   USA

First Printing
June 2007

ISBN: 0-941967-26-3

Old Fort Niagara is a New York State Historic Site operated by
the *Old Fort Niagara Association, Inc.*, in cooperation with, and
under license from, the
*New York State Office of Parks, Recreation and Historic Preserva-
tion.*
The site is a Registered National Historic Landmark.

• A History and Guide to Old Fort Niagara •
(2007 Revised Edition ProductionNotes)

Original Text: *Brian Leigh Dunnigan*
Design, Layout, and Production Coordinator: *Harry M. DeBan*
Word Processing and Text Conversion: *David J. Bertuca*
Proofing: *Robert L. Emerson, John Jacob Ulrich Rivardi, Michel duLac*
Editor: *Harry M. DeBan*

• Old Fort Niagara Publications •
Chairman and Publisher:
Harry M. DeBan

Committee and Editorial Board:
*David J. Bertuca; R. Arthur Bowler; Craig O. Burt, III; David Caldwell,
Harry M. DeBan, Lawrence Fortunato, Patricia Rice.*

Old Fort Niagara: Three Hundred Years of History

Few American historic sites have had such intensive military occupation as the point of land at the mouth of the Niagara River. Here, where the discharge of four Great Lakes flows into Lake Ontario, a flat, slightly elevated peninsula commands the juncture of the waters. For more than three centuries garrisons were maintained and defenses constructed on this spot.

The military post at the mouth of the Niagara has undergone numerous transformations during its three hundred year history. The site proved to be highly adaptable, and it remained occupied while hundreds of other military posts quickly outlived their usefulness and were abandoned. The nations which held this site had specific reasons for expending lives and treasure to maintain a fort at Niagara. Their reasons and the fortifications they constructed differed with technology and the strategic needs of the time. The original, tiny stockade soon gave way to sophisticated eighteenth century fortifications. When those walls in turn became obsolete, during the nineteenth century, they were replaced by an undefended complex of barracks. Today, a United States Coast Guard Station is the last vestige of active military occupation of the site.

The buildings and walls preserved within Old Fort Niagara and Fort Niagara State Park represent many different phases in the development and use of this historic site. Archaeological remains beneath the soil mark the presence of other long vanished features as well as the thousands of soldiers, traders and Native Americans who witnessed the colorful history of the post.

Three nations held Fort Niagara during its long history. Their presence is symbolized by the historical flags which daily fly above the fort's parade ground. The banners of France, Great Britain and the United States recall the turbulence of the struggle for North America.

Louis XIV
King of France

Gateway to the West: The French 1678 – 1759

Throughout much of its history, the importance of Fort Niagara derived from an accident of geography. The connecting basins of the Great Lakes flow south and east into Lake Erie on their way to the sea. At the eastern end of Lake Erie, however, the waters collected from much of the interior of the continent are constricted into the Niagara River. Seventeen miles from Lake Erie the river drops down a series of rapids and takes the fearful plunge over Niagara Falls. Once free of the Cataracts and the Niagara Gorge, the waters enter Ontario, last of the Great Lakes, and eventually flow down the St. Lawrence River to the Atlantic Ocean.

Three hundred years ago this extensive water system, stretching from the Atlantic to central Canada and the American Midwest, provided a natural transportation route through the rugged wilderness. By utilizing the lakes and their numerous tributaries, the Native peoples and European explorers could cross much of the continent. Portages connected the Great Lakes with water systems leading to the Ohio and Mississippi Valleys, the Gulf of Mexico and the Great Plains. These "carrying places" around obstacles to water transport — rapids, heights of land and, of course, Niagara Falls — were the control points for waterborne commerce. The early importance of the Fort Niagara site derived almost solely from the portage around Niagara Falls. Once this portage lost its usefulness, the strategic value of Fort Niagara virtually disappeared.

When European people began settling on the coast of North America in the early seventeenth century, the French accidentally occupied the most convenient route to the interior. From their posts at Quebec and Montreal they rapidly moved up the St. Lawrence River to explore the continent and trade for furs with the Native peoples. Although this route should have led them directly to Niagara and the great Falls, their path was blocked by the hostility of the Native people of the region, the Five Nations of the Iroquois.

The Iroquois consisted of five distinct nations linked by language and culture. By the fifteenth century, however, they had allied in a powerful confederation. This kept internal peace and allowed mutual defense against outsiders. The country of the Five Nations stretched across New York from the Mohawk River to the Niagara. Ranged from east to west were the Mohawk Oneida, Onondaga, Cayuga, and Seneca. These people became known as the six Nations during the eighteenth century when the original five accepted the refugee Tuscarora from North Carolina.

Westernmost of the Iroquois nations was the Seneca. Though after the mid-seventeenth century the Niagara was part of their territory, the Seneca did not heavily populate the area. Their main villages were located in the Genesee Valley, about eighty miles to the east. Archaeological evidence suggests however, that the site of Fort Niagara was used seasonally as a fishing and hunting camp.

The Iroquois, perhaps the most politically powerful group of Native people in the history of North America, had early confrontations with the French. Their hostility would last until the French had been driven from North America. Since much of the land around Lake Ontario was Iroquois country French exploration and influence was at first diverted up the Ottawa River to the northern Great Lakes. Iroquois animosity toward the French was not, however, continuous. Relations between the two peoples fluctuated. These cycles had much influence on French use of the Niagara.

❁ The 1st Fort at Niagara ❁ "Fort Conti"

The first documented visit by Frenchmen to the site of Fort Niagara occurred in 1669 during a period of peaceful relations with the Iroquois. A party of priests and explorers, which included Rene-Robert Cavalier, Sieur de La Salle, passed the elevated point and noted the great river. Nine years later La Salle returned to explore the Niagara and construct a sailing vessel above the Falls.

In order to support his shipbuilding efforts, La Salle required a post at the mouth of the river. Here, vessels crossing Lake Ontario with supplies from Fort Frontenac (modern Kingston, Ontario) could make a landfall. Early in 1679 a party of men constructed a storehouse and a stockade on the later site of Fort Niagara. The post was named Fort Conti after Louis Armand de Bourbon, Prince of Conti, a patron of La Salle's lieutenant, Henri de Tonty. Once La Salle had weighed anchor on Lake Erie in the summer of 1679, however, the men left to guard Fort Conti became careless. A fire consumed the buildings before the end of the year.

❀ The 2nd Fort at Niagara ❀ "Fort Denonville"

The second French post to occupy the site of Fort Niagara was established under less peaceful circumstances. Good relations between the French and the Iroquois ended a few years after the destruction of Fort Conti. By 1687 the Governor of New France, Jacques-Rene de Brisay, Marquis de Denonville, was prepared to strike a blow against the old enemies of New France. Denonville gathered troops and Indian allies in Canada and marched against the Iroquois of Western New York.

Governor Denonville spent the summer of 1687 engaged in an impressive, if futile, campaign against Seneca villages in the Genesee Valley near the site of modern Rochester, New York. Houses and crops were destroyed, but few warriors were captured or killed. To complete his attempt to pacify the Iroquois, Denonville moved his army to the mouth of the Niagara River. There he established a fort. Within a few weeks a stockade enclosing eight buildings had been erected and christened Fort Denonville. Then, leaving one hundred men under Captain Pierre de Troyes to hold the post for the winter, the Governor and his army returned to Montreal.

Fort Denonville, the first truly military outpost on the Niagara River, was sturdily constructed. Its palisades, however, provided little defense against the most sinister enemies: isolation, cold, starvation and disease. Cut off from supplies and reinforcements and surrounded by hostile Senecas, the garrison sickened and died. By April, only twelve soldiers remained alive, including their gravely ill de Troyes.

These few men were saved by a relief force which arrived in the Niagara River on Good Friday, 1688. The horrified reinforcements did what they could for the emaciated survivors. Their chaplain, Jesuit Father Pierre Millet, erected a tall wooden cross in the center of

Louis XV
King of France

Denonville's fort, and offered a Mass of thanksgiving for their survival. Not long after that, he administered "Last Rites" to the dying de Troyes, holding him at the captain's final moment of life.

Fort Denonville was regarrisoned, but the lesson had been learned. The post was too far from the center of New France to be maintained in the face of Iroquois hostility. In September the troops pulled down the stockade and left the buildings to the elements. It would be thirty-eight years before French soldiers again occupied the site.

❧ The French Return ❧

Aside from the embarrassment of retreat from the Iroquois country, the fiasco at Fort Denonville stirred ominous rumblings from a new rival to French control of the Niagara. The Iroquois had originally looked to the Dutch colony of Nieuw Amsterdam for European goods and guns to fight their enemies. Once the English took the Dutch colony, in 1664, they inherited the alliance with the Five Nations. When Denonville's army marched into the Iroquois country, the Governor of New York (as Nieuw Amsterdam had been renamed) protested loudly. The event marked the beginning of a long rivalry for the lands surrounding the Great Lakes. As relations between France and England worsened in Europe, both nations increased their efforts to gain the upper hand in the forests of America. The French thus found control of the Niagara Portage all the more desirable.

The turn of the eighteenth century was marked by open colonial warfare between France and England. King William's War (1689-1697) and Queen Anne's War (1702-1713) also involved the Iroquois and other Indian nations. These conflicts weakened the Iroquois and pushed them toward a more neutral attitude. At the same time France moved to consolidate her position on the Great Lakes. A post constructed at Detroit in 1701 blocked the British from the three northwestern lakes. In 1715 a new fort at Michilimackinac assured their influence in the north. Niagara and its portage was the linchpin, however. Control of it would assure the exclusion of the English from the Great Lakes and the safe movement of goods and furs to and from New France.

French efforts to improve relations with the Iroquois increased during this time. Agents and traders slowly gained influence over the western Iroquois nations, particularly the Seneca. Chief among these men was Louis-Thomas Chabert de Joncaire. In 1720 he gained permission from the Iroquois to establish a trading house on the Niagara Portage. Chabert selected a site at the foot of the Niagara Escarpment. He dubbed his post the "Magazin Royale" and displayed the colors of the French King, a move which, predictably, brought howls of protest from the English. Undeterred, Chabert traded with the Indians and increased his influence among them.

❧ *The 3rd Fort at Niagara* ❧ *The House of Peace & the Foundation of "Fortress Niagara"*

Louis-Thomas Chabert de Joncaire had achieved much for New France. His efforts had finally placed a fort on the Niagara River. It was not, however, a strong post. By itself the Magazin Royale posed little threat to English ambitions. Within a few years, therefore, Chabert was again requesting permission of the Iroquois to construct a trading house on the Niagara. To allay their suspicions he justified the request by promising to construct a place for trade. Termed a "House of Peace," it was not to be a formal military post but, rather, a place where the Iroquois could barter for furs and meet with the representatives of the French King. Permission was granted by the Iroquois in 1725.

Early in June, 1726, a French flotilla arrived at the mouth of the Niagara River. Although their original plan had been to construct a stronger post on the site of the Magazin Royale, Gaspard-Joseph Chaussegros de Lery, the engineer sent to perform the work, soon made a major change. He felt that the point of land at the mouth of the river, site of the vanished buildings of Denonville's fort, provided the best position to control the route to the west. Chaussegros accordingly laid out his post where it could overlook river and lake and face a possible English attack from the East.

The French were faced with a particular problem. While it was necessary to construct fortifications strong enough to resist an attack by the Iroquois or the British, the post could not have the appearance of a true fortification. Chaussegros de Lery's solution was to erect a large stone house surrounded by a simple wooden stockade. Such a building would not be threatening, and yet its walls would be proof against the small arms available to the Iroquois. This was the origin of the "French Castle," oldest of the buildings of Fort Niagara. Chaussegros, however, took pains to avoid calling the building a "castle." He referred to it instead as a "maison a machicoulis" or "machicolated house." The title derived from the overhanging dormers of the second floor which allowed defenders to fire down upon an enemy. In dealings with the Iroquois, however, it was always referred to as the "House of Peace."

Construction of the new fort was nearly complete by the end of 1726. Final touches were added the following year. Regardless of its name, "House of Peace" or "machicolated house," the French finally had a fort at Niagara. Its presence effectively sealed the gateway to the West. The British had access to Lake Ontario from the Oswego River, 150 miles east of the Niagara, but the new French post blocked their route to the other Great Lakes. Establishment of Fort Oswego by the British in 1727 was poor compensation for losing the road to the West.

The House of Peace served the French well as a place to trade with the Indians. A small garrison was also maintained to watch over the portage and protect French interests among the Iroquois. Rivalry with the British continued, but it was not until the 1740's that it again erupted into open conflict. The years of King George's War (1744-1748) saw a growing emphasis on the military value of Fort Niagara. As guardian of the portage the post needed its garrison of about one company of soldiers. The neutrality of the Iroquois prevented a British attack, though it likewise kept the French from using their position at Niagara for attacks on the frontiers of New York. Fort Niagara was expanded during the war, and Chaussegros's old stockade was replaced with new pickets. The larger area within the walls was soon filled with new buildings to supplement the quarters and storerooms available in the French Castle.

❈ *Conflict in the West* ❈

The peace which followed King George's War provided little more than a respite for the climactic struggle to come. The French realized this and used their post at Niagara to prepare for the next conflict. Having secured access to the Great Lakes, they prepared to consolidate their claims to the interior of the continent.

Pierre de Rigaud de Vaudreuil de Cavagnial, Marquis de Vaudreuil (1698-1778), the last Governor General of New France (1755-1760).

King George's War had barely ended when the first of several expeditions gathered at Niagara to establish French domination of the Ohio Valley. In 1749, Celeron de Blainville set out from the post, crossed the portages from Lake Erie to the Ohio, and busied himself with formally claiming possession of that vast area. Further expeditions in the early 1750's used Fort Niagara as the key organization and supply base for the establishment of a chain efforts between Lake Erie and the confluence of the Allegheny and Monongahela Rivers. Conflict with the British over a fort on the latter site (today's Pittsburgh) provided the spark which ignited the last of the major American colonial wars.

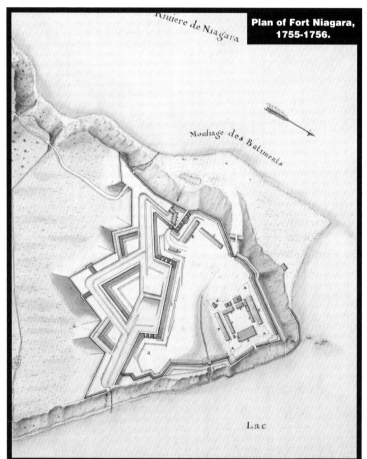

Plan of Fort Niagara, 1755-1756.

With the outbreak of hostilities, Fort Niagara's value redoubled, yet the post remained little more than a rickety frontier stockade. While it might have been formidable to an enemy lacking artillery, the new conflict was certain to bring cannon within range of the walls. Unlike earlier colonial wars, both France and Britain soon committed large numbers of trained regular soldiers to the campaigns in North America. The French and Indian War, as the conflict is popularly known today, would result in the complete transformation of Fort Niagara.

The fighting began with a crushing defeat of British General Edward Braddock in the upper Ohio Valley. However, Fort Niagara, vital link of the victorious French troops with Montreal, was threatened by a second British army when General William Shirley gathered his forces at Oswego, Fort Niagara's old rival, during the summer of 1755. Weakly defended, the post would have fallen quickly had Shirley attacked. He delayed too long, however. Autumn and the threat of cold weather put an end to the campaign season before Shirley could strike.

The lesson was not lost on the French. Niagara was too important to be left in its dilapidated state. In the fall of 1755, a large body of regular troops, recently arrived from France, was sent across Lake Ontario. With them went Captain Pierre Pouchot carrying orders to transform the post and make it defensible against artillery. Pouchot was admirably successful. By the spring of 1756, he had greatly enlarged the fort and constructed new earthwork defenses. The useless old stockade was torn down. The Castle, however, survived as the largest building in the fort. By the end of another year the expanded interior had been filled with new buildings of wood and stone. Barracks, storehouses, a powder magazine, and even a church had been completed.

Pouchot's efforts were aided by French offensive actions which moved the fighting well away from Niagara. Oswego was captured in 1756, thus removing the nearest potential base for a British attack. The next two years would find the Fort Niagara garrison busily supporting Native allies in their raids against the frontiers of Pennsylvania and Virginia.

❅ *The Siege of Fort Niagara* ❅

Throughout this great conflict, the Iroquois (now composed of Six Nations) had remained largely neutral. Their support was courted by both antagonists, but as British strength grew the Iroquois began to turn against the French. The old animosity, lingering bitterness over the presence of a French fort on their territory at Niagara and the persuasiveness of British Indian Superintendent Sir William Johnson finally ended Iroquois neutrality. Their declaration of support, late in 1758, made a British attack on Niagara possible.

The French fully expected such a move. Pressured on all fronts by the more numerous British forces, they did their best to prepare a defense. Captain Pouchot was again assigned to command Niagara. He arrived in April, 1759, with a few reinforcements and orders to hold his post as long as possible. Early in the summer a British army under Brigadier General John Prideaux began moving west from Albany. Part of the force was left at Oswego to rebuild that fort. The remainder, some 2000 soldiers, and 1500 Iroquois warriors led by Johnson himself, set out for the western end of Lake Ontario. On July 6, they landed four miles east of Fort Niagara and laid siege to the post.

The ensuing nineteen days witnessed one of the classic sieges in the history of North America. For more than two weeks the six hundred man French garrison resisted as the British dug trenches toward the walls, constructed batteries for heavy guns and slowly pounded Fort Niagara to pieces. By July 24, the attackers' trenches were only eighty yards from the walls, and the garrison was on the verge of collapse.

Captain Pouchot held on, in part, because he knew help was approaching. Before Fort Niagara was surrounded, he had sent messages to the garrisons of Detroit and the Ohio Valley ordering them to come to his relief. Come they did, 1500 Frenchmen and Indians. On July 23, they started down the Niagara River from Lake Erie hoping to fight their way through the British to the beleaguered garrison.

The British, however, were expecting them. Sir William Johnson, commanding the attackers since the death of General Prideaux on July 20, sent a detachment to block the road leading to the fort. His troops took post a mile up the river at a place known as "La Belle Famille." The next morning the French attacked, charging forward against the British regulars. The redcoats stood their ground, firing repeated, disciplined volleys into the French ranks. Within twenty minutes the battle was over, and the survivors of the shattered relief force were in flight toward Lake Erie. The action was decisive. When Captain Pouchot learned of the rout he asked for surrender terms. On July 25, Fort Niagara became British.

George II
King of Great Britain

Guardhouse of the Great Lakes: The British 1759 – 1796

The hoisting of the Union Jack signaled the beginning of Fort Niagara's period of greatest use and importance. For the next thirty-seven years the post would usually have a substantial garrison, and the commander of Fort Niagara would exercise wide authority over the Great Lakes country.

Although the capture of Niagara did not immediately establish British control of the region, the French lifeline to the West had been severed. The western frontier was therefore relatively quiet for the final year of war. During its first months under British colors, Fort

Enlarged view: Reverse of 1759 British Victory Commemorsative; "1759 The Year of Victories."

Niagara was badly isolated, however. Its only link with the Atlantic colonies was a tenuous route across Lake Ontario and down the Mohawk Valley to Albany and New York. So difficult was it to supply the post after the siege, that inadequate supplies caused a scurvy epidemic among the soldiers of Fort Niagara during the winter of 1759-1760. By spring, 150 men had perished.

The campaign of 1760 ended French resistance in Canada. By autumn, Fort Niagara had become the staging point for parties of British troops moving west to take possession of the posts on the Great Lakes. Thus began British Fort Niagara's role as a supply depot and chief avenue of communication with the Upper Lakes. The movement of supplies would occupy the garrison for many years. Without this vital post, British domination of the Great Lakes would have been impossible.

Fort Niagara also continued to be an important location for meeting with the Native peoples. This was crucial in the years immediately following the conquest of Canada. The tribes of the Lakes had been allies of the French. Undefeated in battle, they were puzzled by the surrender of their lands to the British. In 1761, Sir William Johnson convened a council at Fort Niagara in an attempt to cement relations with the tribes. His efforts might have had more lasting results had other British officials and many fur traders not treated the Indians with contempt.

❧ The Uprising of 1763 – 1764 ❧

Dissatisfaction with the British grew in the early years of the 1760's. By the spring of 1763, Indian resentment had erupted into a full scale revolt. In less than two months, the tribes of the Great Lakes attacked and captured eight small posts scattered from Pennsylvania to Wisconsin. Only Detroit and Fort Pitt (Pittsburgh) withstood the onslaught. The revolt, today often called the "Pontiac Uprising" (after the Ottawa chief who led the attack on Detroit), put tremendous strain on British forces in America, and reemphasized the value of the fort and portage at Niagara.

When news of the outbreak of hostilities and the plight of Detroit reached Fort Niagara, all energies were turned to supplying and reinforcing the beleaguered post. Detroit was well fortified, and its garrison had little to fear from a direct assault. Starvation might force surrender, however. The movement of supplies and reinforcements over the Niagara Portage, therefore, became a paramount concern.

Efforts to support Detroit continued, with considerable success, throughout the summer of 1763. Although it proved impossible to suppress the uprising, the garrison held the fort. The Indians were well aware of the important role of the Niagara Portage and soon resolved to attack it. Though Fort Niagara was too strong to be seriously threatened, the Portage Road itself was long and weakly defended. On September 14, 1763, a large party of Senecas ambushed a train of wagons near a natural feature of the Niagara Gorge known as "Devil's Hole." An attempt to save the wagons resulted in the ambush of the relief force and the most costly defeat of the war for the British. Worst of all, valuable draft animals and vehicles were destroyed by the Senecas. Although these losses were replaced within a few weeks, the ambush at Devil's Hole seriously interrupted efforts to supply Detroit. Winter found the two sides at an impasse. The Indians were still unable to capture Detroit, but the British had been equally unsuccessful in quelling the rebellion.

During the winter, the British laid plans for ending the war. A pair of expeditions would penetrate the Indian country in 1764 and force the tribes to sue for peace. The northern prong, under the command of Colonel John Bradstreet, was to gather at Niagara to relieve Detroit and end the war on the Great Lakes. While the military force prepared for the campaign, Sir William Johnson invited the Indians of the Upper Lakes to Niagara for a grand council in the early summer of 1764. The most hostile groups did not respond to Johnson's invitation. Those who had not participated in the rebellion or who had become disillusioned by the war, appeared in great numbers, however. During July, the grounds outside Fort Niagara presented a colorful scene, as warriors of many different nations reaffirmed their friendship for the British. Those who did not attend were considered hostile, and subject to attack by the army.

Bradstreet's troops spent much of the summer carrying supplies across the Niagara Portage and preparing for their journey to Detroit. They also expended much effort fortifying the portage to prevent a recurrence of the Devil's Hole disaster. Finally, before embarking for Detroit, the army constructed a new post on the shore of Lake Erie. This stockade at the head of the Niagara River was christened "Fort Erie."

George III
King of Great Britain

Bradstreet's expedition encountered no outright resistance on its way to Detroit. Though the operation was something of an anticlimax, it reestablished control of the Upper Great Lakes. The British had been badly shaken by the uprising, however, and their relations with the Indians would thereafter be guarded.

Efforts to maintain the defenses of Fort Niagara over the next ten years were clearly aimed at the Indians as the potential enemy. This is hardly surprising. With the French expelled from America, there was no European adversary to threaten the post, the Great Lakes or Canada. The decade following the Indian uprising thus saw a steady decline in the condition of the fortifications. The lack of a serious threat to the post, combined with efforts by the British to reduce military expenditures in America, resulted in smaller garrisons. There was likewise unwillingness to lavish funds on the fortifications. The once impressive earthworks of Fort Niagara were allowed to crumble. The only part of the defenses carefully maintained was the wooden picketing which protected the post from a surprise attack by the Indians. When major new work was finally authorized in 1768 and again in 1770, it too was aimed at Native Americans. Erection of a stockade around the French Castle in the former year provided a citadel in case of attack. The two stone redoubts begun in the latter were intended as advance posts to protect the new stockade. By 1775, however, the once formidable earthen walls and ditches had almost ceased to exist. Though the buildings were in reasonable repair and the post was well garrisoned, it was far from prepared for the turmoil to come.

❈ The American Revolution ❈

A new rebellion, this time by the colonists of the Atlantic seaboard, erupted in the spring of 1775. The eight year war which followed would cause many changes at Niagara. By the end of the conflict the simple frontier military post would be no more, and the post commanders would have many new concerns and responsibilities.

It is ironic that the War for American Independence placed the British garrison of Niagara in a position nearly identical to that of the French two decades before. The British found themselves concerned about defending Canada and controlling access to the Great Lakes. Fort Niagara and the portage would, therefore, serve much the same purpose for the British during the American Revolution as it had for their enemies during the French and Indian War. The post's garrison guarded the route to the Lakes, protected trade (which continued despite the war) and supported military operations in the West. Fort Niagara was also the main point of contact between the British and the Iroquois.

Unlike the French, however, the British enjoyed the almost unreserved support of the Six Nations of the Iroquois, as well as that of many colonists who were opposed to the rebellion. Both groups of people would become refugees, and both would actively engage in military operations on behalf of King George III. Niagara became a safe haven for these "Loyalists" and a base for their retaliatory operations. Fort Niagara is, in fact, most often remembered in American history as the base of raiders who terrorized the frontiers of New York and Pennsylvania. The Canadian perspective is much different. In their view, the post was a bastion of loyalty and the avenue to a new life in Canada.

The war took a while to reach Niagara. During the summer and fall of 1775, "Rebel" forces struck north along Lake Champlain, and overran much of Canada. Their operations took place far from Fort Niagara, but the American successes isolated the post from England and much needed supplies. It was not until nearly a year later that the invaders were driven south by British reinforcements, and the supply route up the St. Lawrence River reopened.

By 1777, Niagara was actively involved in the war as a base for offensive operations. That year's unsuccessful British expedition against the Mohawk Valley included soldiers from Niagara. Although their effort to support General John Burgoyne's Saratoga campaign foundered on stubborn American resistance at Fort Stanwix (Rome, New York), it signaled the beginning of Fort Niagara's role as nemesis of the frontier settlements.

The winter of 1777-1778 saw growing activity at Fort Niagara, as John Butler, a prominent Mohawk Valley Loyalist, began recruiting and organizing a military unit of his fellow refugees. "Butler's Rangers" would eventually grow to a full regiment and serve throughout the war at Niagara and on the Great Lakes-New York frontier. Their devastating raids, in company with warriors of the Six Nations, created panic on the frontier and earned them a fearful reputation in the folklore of the American Revolution. The actions of Butler's men were, however, only representative of a wilderness war which grew increasingly bitter as it progressed. The Rangers, in fact, were raiding their former neighbors and political adversaries. Atrocities would be committed by both sides during the long conflict to come.

Butler first led his Rangers and Six Nations allies into action during 1778. His raid against the Wyoming Valley of Pennsylvania (July) and his son Walter's attack on the New York settlement of Cherry Valley (November) were unqualified victories for the raiders from Niagara. Their successes, and the cruel fate of many of the settlers, triggered an American reaction which would greatly escalate the conflict on the frontier.

The Continental Congress was well aware of the danger of these backwoods attacks. The farms of New York and Pennsylvania, deep in American territory, were important sources of supply for the Continental Army. Raiders from Niagara were in a position to harass the

population from the rear, and the disruption of the farms could have serious effects on the already strained American military situation. The forts which guarded the farthest settlements had proved ineffective in stopping the raids. Indians and Rangers were able to strike the frontiers almost at will, and some groups even marched eastward from Niagara as far as New Jersey. An offensive stroke was considered necessary to punish the Six Nations for their allegiance to the King, and to counter the raids from Niagara.

During the summer of 1779, a large part of the Continental Army was detached for service in the West. General John Sullivan gathered the main body in Pennsylvania. General James Clinton assembled a second force in the Mohawk Valley of New York. Employing the river systems, the two detachments of experienced troops joined and marched into the Iroquois country. Sullivan's troops soon found themselves among the Six Nations villages of Western New York. The Indians and their British allies were unable to effectively counter the overwhelming American numbers. The Continentals were, in fact, able to march to within eighty miles of Fort Niagara.

In consternation, the British frantically attempted to reinforce the post, repair its defenses, and provide it with supplies to withstand a siege. Sullivan was well aware of his limitations, however. Far from his base, lacking supplies and heavy artillery and with winter approaching, he was in no position to seriously threaten Fort Niagara. Satisfied with the destruction of many Iroquois villages and a large part of their corn crop and orchards, he retired to Pennsylvania. This was the closest approach of American troops to Niagara during the war.

Though Sullivan's men had encountered few warriors, they had dealt the Iroquois a severe blow. With their food supplies destroyed, the Six Nations had little choice but to gather at Niagara and rely on British support. Unfortunately, the post was in no position to feed so many extra mouths. By the time the extent of the destruction became known, it was too late in the season to transport extra supplies to Niagara. Though some of the Iroquois were dispersed to the few undamaged villages, the winter of 1779-1780 was an extremely harsh and hungry one for most of the Native refugees huddled in camps near Fort Niagara.

Sullivan's expedition was destructive, but it did not knock the Six Nations out of the war. Spring found raiding parties again striking at the frontiers and supporting British expeditions sent from the posts on Lake Ontario. Niagara would continue its role as a raiding base for the remainder of the war.

The years following 1779 also saw Fort Niagara become increasingly important to the widening conflict in the West. Detroit and Michilimackinac were strongholds of British authority on the Great Lakes. They were seriously threatened by the growing American presence in Kentucky and the Ohio Valley, and even by the Spanish on the Mississippi. Detroit was particularly valuable, and raids from that post harried Kentucky frontiersmen throughout the war. Not surprisingly, Detroit was a major target of American forces. The commander of Fort Niagara, who also controlled all British forces on the Upper Great Lakes, thus had to be concerned about the security of that settlement. The relatively large garrison of Fort Niagara served a pivotal role, prepared to oppose attacks from the East or to reinforce Detroit. Fort Niagara was also an important intelligence gathering center. Small parties of Rangers were constantly in the field, spying on enemy forces. It was not uncommon for the Governor of Canada to receive news of major military events on the Atlantic seaboard from Niagara, well ahead of reports sent by sea.

Throughout this time, Fort Niagara was the destination of many Loyalists fleeing the western parts of the former colonies. Many made their way through the wilderness, at great peril. Once safely at Niagara, the women and children were sent to Canada, while the men reinforced the ranks of Butler's Rangers. Fort Niagara was also the unwilling destination of hundreds of captives taken on the frontiers by Iroquois raiders. Contrary to popular belief, the British went to considerable effort and expense to ransom these people. Like the noncombatant Loyalists, the prisoners were sent to Montreal.

❈ The Holdover Period ❈

The War for Independence began sputtering to a halt after the 1781 defeat, at Yorktown, of Lord Cornwallis. Hostilities on the frontier continued for another year, however. British forces occupied Oswego, and rebuilt its ruined fort in 1782 to provide a buffer against American incursions into the lands of the Six Nations. This action also protected Niagara. By 1783, however, peace negotiations had advanced to the point where the British ceased attacks against the frontier, and urged their Indian allies to do likewise. Late in the year, news arrived of the cessation of hostilities and the ratification of a peace treaty.

The terms of the Treaty of Paris were shocking to the British and Loyalist officers who had defended Fort Niagara throughout the war. The boundary between the new United States and British Canada was drawn through the Great Lakes, following much the same route as the modern border. Fort Niagara and many of the other posts of the Lakes fell on the American side of the line. Worst of all, the lands of the Six Nations were placed well within the boundaries of their former enemies.

The officers at Niagara were so disturbed that, at first, they attempted to keep this news from the Iroquois, for fear of retaliation against British and Loyalist forces. In less than a year, however, it became clear that the British would retain the Great Lakes posts, at least for a while. Disputes over the treaty provided an excuse to delay the transfer of the forts. American soldiers, merchants, and settlers thus remained barred from the lakes by British garrisons. The tribes retained their loyalties to the British, and preparations for transferring the forts at Carleton Island, Oswego, Niagara, Detroit and Michilimackinac were halted.

With Niagara still safely under their control, the British turned their attention to resettling the refugee Loyalists. The vast area of modern Ontario provided land for many new villages and farms. By 1784 discharged Loyalist soldiers and their families were receiving land grants around Lake Ontario. Many of the men of Butler's Rangers took up property on the west side of the Niagara River. Though the early years were difficult, the new settlements prospered within a decade. The development of the west bank contrasted sharply with the east side of the river which remained wilderness. Despite the temporary delay, the British knew that Fort Niagara and the adjacent territory would eventually be ceded to the United States.

Resolution of the dispute over the Great Lakes posts took eleven years. By 1794, however, the British were fully involved in a new European war, and an enlarged United States Army was moving against the Indians of the Ohio country. A new conflict in North America would have been disastrous for Britain. The time was ripe for negotiation, and the Jay Treaty was signed that year. It guaranteed that the posts would be turned over to the United States. The transfer was accomplished in the summer of 1796. United States troops marched through the gates of Fort Niagara in August, and raised the Stars and Stripes above the ramparts.

George Washington
1st President of the United States

A Defended Border: The Americans 1796-1872

The situation of Fort Niagara changed drastically the moment United States soldiers took possession of the post. Originally intended to dominate the mouth of the river and control the portage, Fort Niagara had suddenly become a border fortification. Potentially hostile territory was now located only six hundred yards away. The former British garrison had withdrawn just across the river, and the nearest American post was at Oswego, 150 miles to the east. The new garrison of Fort Niagara must have felt terribly isolated. Even worse, their fortifications, which had been designed to guard against a land attack, now literally faced the wrong way.

Despite this new situation, the first in which two powers faced each other across the Niagara River, some of the functions of Fort Niagara remained unchanged. The portage around Niagara Falls was as important to the Americans as it had been for the French and the British. Though Fort Niagara was no longer the only post along the river, it was still well placed to protect the beginning of the carrying place. The old portage route on the east bank was taken over by the Americans. In 1790, anticipating the arrival of United States soldiers, the British had established a new road on the west side of the river. Throughout the early years of the nineteenth century the two portages operated opposite each other.

The lonely garrison of Fort Niagara was isolated for only a short time. In the first years of the nineteenth century, the lands on the New York side of the Niagara River were surveyed. They rapidly filled with settlers. By the end of the first decade of the century, thriving villages had been established along the frontier at Youngstown, Lewiston, Manchester, Schlosser (the last two now part of the city of Niagara Falls), Black Rock, and Buffalo. Protection of this civilian population presented an additional responsibility for the garrison of Fort Niagara. The soldiers assisted with development as well. In 1803-1804, work parties from Fort Niagara constructed a military road from the top of the Niagara Escarpment at Lewiston, to Black Rock (now a part of

Buffalo). This road, which greatly aided settlement of the area and by-passed much of the old portage route, still exists as New York Route 265.

While the Americans consolidated their hold on the New York side of the Niagara, the British constructed a new fort across the river. Fort George was completed by 1799, on high ground just south of the modern village of Niagara-on-the-Lake. Though not as stoutly constructed as Fort Niagara, it stood on higher ground where its guns could dominate the American position. Despite such military preparations, however, relations between the two garrisons were surprisingly cordial. The bitterness of the American Revolution was softening somewhat, and the professional officers of the two posts were eager to socialize. Officers from the American garrison attended church on the British side of the river. British doctors even occasionally cared for the soldiers of Fort Niagara during the absence of the American surgeon.

Unfortunately, relations became strained once more, as the first decade of the nineteenth century progressed. Tensions resulted from British disregard for American neutrality and maritime rights, as well as Yankee designs on Canada. Outright conflict was, perhaps, inevitable. In June, 1812, the United States declared war on Great Britain.

❀ *The War of 1812* ❀

Fort Niagara was woefully unprepared for war. The fortifications had again deteriorated during the decade after 1800, as the garrison became increasingly smaller. Many of the old buildings, some of them relics of the French occupation, disappeared during those years. The land-side walls remained in place, but the garrison could provide few workmen to keep them in good condition. At the outbreak of hostilities, the Americans could muster only 150 men at Fort Niagara.

If United States forces along the Niagara Frontier were unprepared for war, so too were their British adversaries. The demands of the Napoleonic Wars in Europe meant that Canada could be only weakly guarded. There were, in 1812, only two thousand British regular soldiers in all of Upper Canada (today's Ontario). Although supplemented by the Canadian militia, the number of troops was far fewer than that which could be assembled by the United States.

This disparity of forces proved to be of less importance than it at first appeared. The bulk of the United States Army was composed of newly organized units filled with untrained recruits. Many senior American leaders were equally inexperienced, or had last seen action thirty years earlier during the American Revolution. The vast numbers of militia, so impressive on paper, proved virtually worthless in the field. American troops, initially confident that they need only march into the major Canadian cities, found a more difficult conflict than they had anticipated. Some of the bloodiest fighting would occur along the Niagara River.

Fort Niagara's tiny garrison prepared for a British assault as soon as they learned of the declaration of war. Short of artillery, supplies and soldiers, Captain Nathaniel Leonard did what he could to improve his defenses. A British attack failed to materialize, however, because they too feared attack, and concentrated on organizing a defense. Much of the summer was spent in preparation, as units of New York Militia were called into service and marched to the Niagara Frontier. In order to avoid friction between officers of the militia and the regular army, the militia established their camp at Lewiston, six miles up the river. Fort Niagara was left in the hands of its regular garrison, soon augmented by new arrivals.

Aside from all this frantic preparation, the summer and early fall of 1812 proved to be a quiet time on the Niagara Frontier. The local commanders soon arranged a truce in order to strengthen their respective positions. Though this gained time to gather forces, the more numerous American troops thereby lost the initiative. Worse, the truce allowed the British to transfer soldiers to the West and achieve an important victory at Detroit in August.

By the time the truce expired in October, the British forces had returned to their Niagara positions. Though still outnumbered, they were prepared for a defensive action. They did not have long to wait. On October 13, 1812, United States troops began crossing the river from Lewiston, and landing at the Canadian village of Queenston. Originally planned to include United States regulars and New York Militia, the operation was soon jeopardized when the militia refused to leave the bounds of the United States! Many of the regulars had already crossed the treacherous river and established a beachhead on the opposite shore. Unsupported, they achieved initial success and struck the British a heavy blow by killing their capable commander, General Isaac Brock. The isolated Americans were unable to withstand a British counterattack, however, and the troops on the Canadian bank of the river were forced to surrender.

Hand colored engraving of "Betsy Doyle" helping load hot-shot into a cannon during bombardment of Fort George, November 1812.

Old Fort Niagara Archives.

Fort Niagara played its own part in this hard fought battle. The garrison was ordered to create a diversion by commencing a bombardment of Fort George. The fire was returned, and a brisk exchange ensued. The vulnerability of Fort Niagara became painfully apparent during this action. Although the American gunners caused damage to the enemy post, the heavy return fire eventually drove them from their positions and caused Fort Niagara to be abandoned. With its batteries silenced and the garrison huddled outside the walls, the post was exposed to a British assault. Realizing this, the American officers gathered a group of volunteers and reoccupied the fort. The British, their resources stretched to the limit by the fighting raging at Queenston, made no attempt to cross the river and take Fort Niagara.

Although quiet returned to the Frontier following the Battle of Queenston Heights, Fort Niagara was the scene of much work, as United States Engineers attempted to improve the old fortifications. The exposed river side of the fort was strengthened with temporary walls. The greatest problem, however, was caused by the fact that Fort George stood on higher ground than the American post. In an at-

Segment from painting (Battle of Chippewa) by H. Charles McBarron. Courtesy, US Army Center of Military History.

American Regulars at the Battle of Chippewa, wearing the uniform jackets which were to give rise to "The Long Gray Line" of the US Military Academy at West Point, NY, where cadets don gray uniforms, honoring the regulars at Chippewa & Lundy's Lane during the War of 1812, who wore the rough gray kersey of the New York militia, because the Army lacked sufficient regulation federal blue.

tempt to counter this advantage, the roofs were removed from the two Redoubts and the "French Castle." Cannon were then mounted on the upper floors. This improved the gunners' effectiveness in returning the fire of the British batteries.

The alterations to Fort Niagara came just in time. On November 21, the guns of Fort George opened fire once again. On this occasion the Americans gave better than they got, though it was still clear that the old fort was badly exposed to the Canadian shore. The action of November 21 gave Fort Niagara a heroine as well. At the height of the battle, a cannon mounted on the roof of the French Castle lost one of its crewmen. Into the gap stepped a soldier's wife, Betsy Doyle, who served the gun with great courage and skill.

Active military operations at Niagara ceased with the onset of winter. Both sides spent the season preparing for the spring campaign. For the garrison of Fort Niagara this meant additional drill and training, and much labor on fortifications. The defenses were further improved. Five batteries for heavy guns were also constructed along the riverbank, upstream from Fort Niagara, where they could fire on Fort George.

The spring of 1813 proved to be a momentous time along the Niagara Frontier. After disappointing performance on most fronts during 1812, United States forces, by now better equipped and trained, successfully took the offensive. It was a difficult year for the British in Upper Canada, and would prove to be the high water mark for the Americans.

The campaign on Lake Ontario began in April, when United States naval vessels sailed from Sackets Harbor on the eastern end of the lake. On board the men-of-war was an army commanded by General Henry Dearborn. This powerful force made short work of York (present day, Toronto), capital of Upper Canada, on April 27. The squadron then crossed the lake to the mouth of the Niagara River. There, combining with the troops already assigned to the Niagara Frontier, Dearborn's army prepared for an attack on Fort George.

On May 25-26, 1813, the guns of Fort Niagara and its detached batteries, joined by the fleet, commenced an all-out bombardment of Fort George. The British gunners resisted valiantly, but their batteries were silenced and the wooden buildings of Fort George were burned to the ground. On the morning of May 27, the fleet anchored off the mouth of the river. Following another cannonade, waves of troop-filled boats headed for the beach. Once ashore, the American soldiers encountered fierce resistance from disciplined British regulars. By the end of the day, however, the smoldering remains of Fort George had fallen, and the British were retreating westward along Lake Ontario. For the first time, the mouth of the Niagara River was entirely in American hands.

Unfortunately for the United States troops, this auspicious beginning did not indicate what was to come. Once in control of Fort George the American leadership began to waver. The British army was not pursued, and was thus able to escape and regroup. By the time American troops left Fort George to attack the British, their forces were too few and too late. The invaders were attacked and defeated at Stoney Creek on June 6, and Beaver Dams on June 24. The momentum of the American army was irretrievably lost, and the troops were soon bottled up in the forts at the mouth of the river, subject to disease and boredom, and growing increasingly dispirited.

As autumn neared, American strength at Fort George was further reduced by troop transfers, as the offensive effort of the United States Army shifted to the eastern end of Lake Ontario. By autumn, the defense of the Niagara area was largely in the hands of the New York Militia. In December, their commander, General George McClure, decided that Fort George was untenable. He ordered a withdrawal to the New York side of the river. Fort George was then ordered destroyed to prevent its use by the British. McClure greatly exceeded his instructions, however, and gave an unfortunate second order — the adjacent town of Newark (or Niagara-on-the-Lake) was also to be burned. Private property was destroyed and civilians were left without shelter. This unwarranted and destructive action would lead to British retaliation, and result, by war's end, in the nearly complete devastation of both sides of the Niagara River.

❊ The Capture of Fort Niagara ❊
19 December 1813 . . . Payback in Cold Steel

The British did not delay in exploiting the withdrawal of United States forces. Most of the New York Militia, their terms of service expired, had returned to their homes. The few regular troops still on the Niagara Frontier were concentrated at Fort Niagara and Buffalo. Within a matter of days, the British had planned an assault on Fort Niagara.

On the night of December 18-19, 1813, red-coated soldiers marched up the river from the newly reoccupied ruins of Fort George and crossed to the New York shore. Landing at a place called Five Mile Meadows, they advanced silently down the River Road in the wintry dark. In the village of Youngstown the British encountered a detachment of American soldiers serving as pickets for the garrison. These men had retreated into the houses of the village to escape the cold. British soldiers burst into the houses and ended resistance before a shot could be fired. With this obstacle removed, the 562 man assault force continued a mile further to Fort Niagara.

The United States garrison had been expecting an attack ever since the abandonment of Fort George. On this night, however, their guard was lax. Most of the garrison was asleep, and the commander, Captain Nathaniel Leonard was visiting his family in Lewiston! Just before dawn on the 19th, the British advance party appeared suddenly at the fort gate, at the moment it had been opened to allow a sentry detail to pass. A British sergeant, unrecognized in the darkness, approached the gate closely enough to wedge it open with his body. Within moments the attackers were streaming through the gate. The sleeping members of the garrison had little opportunity to resist. Only a few men in the "Red Barracks" and the guard detail in the South Redoubt were able to organize. Their resistance was fierce. Though the Red Barracks was soon cleared at the point of the bayonet, the South Redoubt was a tougher objective. A party of British soldiers finally broke down the door and fought up two flights of stairs to subdue the sixty-five stubborn defenders. Fort Niagara's garrison of 433 soldiers had lost 65 killed and 15 wounded (15 more were reported killed, according to eyewitness Robert Lee). The unfortunate Captain Leonard arrived at the gate the next morning to find British sentries in control. Only captivity in Canada prevented his trial for treason by the US Army.

The loss of Fort Niagara was only the first in a series of disasters for the Niagara Frontier. On December 19, the British marched from their newly won post and, partly in retaliation for the destruction of Newark, burned the village of Youngstown. Continuing up the River Road, they drove off an American detachment at Lewiston, and destroyed that town as well. By the end of the year, the same fate had befallen Manchester, Schlosser, Black Rock and Buffalo. The New Year found the American side of the Niagara a scorched ruin.

Aside from these destructive forays, the British made no further effort to occupy the countryside around Fort Niagara. By holding the post itself, they dominated the mouth of the river and provided a safe haven for warships and supply vessels. The Union Jack flying over the post was also a powerful political symbol. It meant that a small part of United States territory was in British hands, and provided a potential bargaining chip at the peace table.

The British made a number of improvements and repairs to Fort Niagara during the seventeen months they held the post. It was inevitable that the fort would be returned to the Americans, however. The Treaty of Ghent officially ended the war late in 1814. Its terms called for a return to the "status quo ante bellum," and by the spring of 1815, the two sides were preparing to exchange captured territory and withdraw to their pre-war positions.

❈ *The Americans Return* ❈

United States troops peacefully reoccupied Fort Niagara on May 22, 1815. The British retired once again to their old position at Fort George, now in ruins, and a new post, Fort Mississauga, begun at the mouth of the river in 1814. Though tensions remained, life rapidly returned to normal along the Niagara Frontier. The burned villages and farms were repaired and commerce resumed along the portage.

Fort Niagara had deteriorated badly during the war. Battle damage and a lack of maintenance had resulted in the destruction of many of the old buildings. The few new structures completed by the wartime garrisons provided adequate quarters for a detachment. However, Fort Niagara had begun to assume its modern appearance with a large open parade ground, and the buildings clustered around the walls.

The primary lesson learned about Fort Niagara during the War of 1812 was that it was terribly vulnerable to cannon fire from the Canadian shore. In 1816, the first of several nineteenth century designs was drawn up in an attempt to counter this disadvantage. The plans called for substantial new walls on the river side. The vast expense and improving relations with Great Britain combined to halt the project, virtually as soon as it had begun. Unrepaired, the fortifications continued to deteriorate. By the 1820's, in fact, there was not even a wall along the river side of the fort, and the interior was completely exposed to fire from Fort Mississauga. Peace was Fort Niagara's chief defense.

The 1820's were, in fact, a very peaceful time along the Niagara. The garrison of Fort Niagara was small, though it still served to guard the portage route around Niagara Falls. A similar garrison faced the American troops from the opposite shore. It was during this quiet time that Fort Niagara figured prominently in an important event of medical history. In May, 1825, Army Surgeon William Beaumont arrived from Fort Mackinac, Michigan Territory, to assume command of the post hospital. He was accompanied by a young French Canadian voyageur named Alexis St. Martin. Three years earlier, St. Martin had been terribly wounded in his side by a shotgun blast. The man had remained Beaumont's patient since the accident, and the doctor had noticed a curious development. Though St. Martin had recovered, the wound to his stomach had not closed. Beaumont was thus provided with a unique opportunity to observe the human digestive system at work. His first series of pioneering experiments commenced at Fort Niagara late in the summer of 1825. More sophisticated tests were conducted at other posts during the 1830's. These would result in publication of the first detailed observations on the functioning of the human stomach, and earn Beaumont a place in medical history.

Another event in 1825 had more direct consequences for Fort Niagara. After years of construction, the Erie Canal was completed. This artificial waterway cut across New York, and connected the Great Lakes with the Atlantic Ocean. Buffalo was the western terminus, and completion of the canal started the town on its development as the commercial capital of Western New York. The results were not so fortunate for the merchants of Youngstown and Lewiston, and the operators of the Niagara Portage. In one stroke, the Erie Canal ended nearly two hundred years of commercial through-traffic along the Niagara River. It also did away with the United States Army's chief reasons for maintaining a post at the river's mouth. Within one year, the army had decided to abandon Fort Niagara. The troops were withdrawn, and the buildings and fortifications placed in the hands of a caretaker.

❈ The Morgan Incident ❈

Soon after the departure of the Fort Niagara garrison, the vacant post figured in one of the most bizarre and mysterious events of New York history. Accounts disagree on details and results, and the true story might never be known, since the incident was so politically volatile. In 1826, William Morgan, a resident of Batavia, New York, became disillusioned with Freemasonry. Morgan published a booklet exposing the secrets of the order, and thus incurred the wrath of the Masons of Western New York.

On September 12, 1826, Morgan was kidnapped and carried to the Niagara Frontier. After much discussion on how best to silence him, someone suggested that Morgan be detained at Fort Niagara. The post's caretaker and its only other resident, a ferryman, were both active Masons. Morgan was locked in the empty Powder Magazine of the fort.

What happened next is still a mystery. The kidnappers soon disagreed about the severity of the measures required to silence and punish Morgan. One faction called for his death, while another felt that matters had already gone too far. Whatever the result of their debate, Morgan disappeared from the Powder Magazine and was never heard from again. Anti-Masons charged that he had been murdered. Masons countered that Morgan had been bribed to leave the country. The ensuing investigations did little to solve the mystery. The only clear result was an aggravation of the already strong anti-Masonic sentiment in New York and the United States.

❊ *The Rebellion of 1837* ❊

Despite the diminished strategic value of Fort Niagara, troops regarrisoned the post in 1828. They did little more than routine duty until 1837, when a rebellion broke out in Canada. The Canadian rebels sought arms, assistance and sanctuary in the United States. The Niagara Frontier saw much activity during this time, including several incidents which aggravated tensions along the border. The British response was to strengthen garrisons and defenses along the Niagara. The walls of Fort Niagara were virtually in ruin, and the activity on the Canadian shore finally prompted action at the old post.

Between 1839 and 1843, laborers under the direction of an officer of the Corps of Engineers, made extensive alterations and additions to buildings and fortifications at Fort Niagara. A heavy stone wall was erected along the river side, to shield the interior of the fort from guns in Fort Mississauga. A seawall was built, and successfully arrested years of erosion by Lake Ontario. Emplacements for heavy guns, a shot furnace, new timber revetments for the land side earthworks, and improvements to the stone buildings completed the project. Though its garrison remained small, Fort Niagara was once again a respectable fortification.

Hand colored engraving, Fort Niagara c. 1835, showing the river front totally defenseless.

Old Fort Niagara Archives.

The end of the Canadian Rebellion eased border tensions, and Fort Niagara's new defenses were not tested. The United States government, in fact, had doubts about the worth of retaining a garrison at the fort. Other priorities, particularly the expanding commitment to the West, often called troops away from Fort Niagara. The post was once more abandoned from 1846 to 1848, while the army was fully involved in the Mexican War. Though soldiers returned in 1848, they were withdrawn again in 1854.

❈ The Civil War ❈

Fort Niagara was reoccupied in 1861, shortly after the outbreak of the War Between the States. Ironically, the post was not at first considered important to the war effort. The enemy was far to the south, and a Confederate attack on Western New York was unlikely. The regular soldiers who regarrisoned Fort Niagara were assigned there only because they could not be used elsewhere. The 7th United States Infantry Regiment had been forced to surrender to the Confederates at Mesilla, New Mexico, on July 25, 1861. Following common practice, the prisoners were paroled on their promise not to fight again until formally exchanged. After their return to the North, the companies of the 7th Infantry were stationed at border posts, far from the front. One detachment occupied Fort Niagara. Exchange for these men finally came in 1863. The troops then joined the war, and Fort Niagara was once again without a garrison.

Old Fort Niagara Archives.

Civil War era color lithograph, used as a Union recruiting poster.

By the time the 7th Infantry departed Fort Niagara, new interest had been focused on the ancient post. Fear that Great Britain might intervene on the side of the Confederacy once again raised tensions on the border. By 1863, plans were afoot to reconstruct fortifications along the Canadian border. Grand designs were drawn for Fort Niagara, and work commenced during the summer of 1863. New revetments to sup-

The Castle and Bakehouse of Fort Niagara during the 1860's are shown in this engraving by Benson J. Lossing, which appeared in his "Pictorial Field Book the War of 1812," printed in 1869.

port the earthen walls of the land front were the first part of the project. Later work was to include new walls and gun positions on the river and lake sides.

Though renovations continued from 1863 to 1872, the Civil War had demonstrated the vulnerability of masonry forts to artillery of the time. Gradually, the ambitious plans were altered. By the time work ceased in 1872, only the land front had been completed. Even then, the new gun positions were not armed, and the walls were obsolescent by the time of their completion.

The fact that work was carried even to this point was probably due to another period of border tension. The threat of British involvement in the Civil War soon disappeared, as Confederate fortunes declined. With the end of hostilities, however, large numbers of discharged veteran Union soldiers of Irish birth became involved in the Fenian movement. Their goal was independence for Ireland. One scheme to achieve this, called for the invasion and conquest of British Canada as a blow against the British Empire and a bargaining chip to gain Ireland's freedom.

Fenian forces gathered at Buffalo in the spring of 1866. In June, an armed force crossed the Upper Niagara River, occupied the village of Fort Erie and defeated Canadian Militia at the Battle of Ridgeway, Ontario. The Fenians, faced with gathering British and Canadian resistance, soon withdrew to Buffalo. United States authorities blocked further raids along the Niagara. Fenian activities continued into the early 1870's, however, and friction between the neighboring nations remained high.

"Defending Forts" 1939
Mural Panel, Officers' Club

Mural: "DEFENDING FORTS," by Eugene Dyczkowski, 1939 WPA/FAP project (Works Progress Administration/Federal Art Project); individual figure panel.

New Fort Niagara: The Americans 1872 – 1963

Fort Niagara was reoccupied by United States soldiers in the fall of 1865. Though the garrison was not directly involved in the Fenian incident, they were useful in guarding the nervous border. The arriving garrison found the fort's accommodations to be primitive and in poor repair. This, combined with the fact that the fortifications themselves were now of questionable value, would cause a significant change in the appearance and use of Fort Niagara.

Almost as soon as the army returned to Fort Niagara, they began to construct new garrison buildings outside the walls. The first of these structures was a hospital. This was followed by company barracks in 1868, and officers' quarters and other structures in 1870. While some construction also occurred within the old walls, future activity would, for the most part, focus on the military reserve east of the fort. This was the beginning of "New" Fort Niagara. By the mid 1880's, most garrison activity was concentrated in that part of the post. The old buildings were employed chiefly for storage or excess accommodations.

The growth of New Fort Niagara followed a number of phases. The first construction of 1865-1870 was followed by major expansions in 1885, 1892, 1908 and 1912. The 1885 work included installation of a 1000 yard rifle range. This would be an important feature of the post, until it was finally abandoned by the army. As New Fort Niagara expanded, the function of the post changed again. With the old fortifications of no further use, the garrison of the 1870's and 1880's was primarily a caretaker detachment, though the post was also used to detain military convicts. Following installation of the rifle range, however, Fort Niagara came into increasing use as a training base.

❄ The "Modern Wars" ❄

With the outbreak of the Spanish-American War in 1898, the regular garrison was called to active service in Cuba. Within a year, how-

Training Camp, 1899, prior to departure for the Philipinnes, 42nd Regt. US Vols.

Old Fort Niagara Archives.

Training Camp, World War One.

Old Fort Niagara Archives.

Temporary Barracks, World War One.

Old Fort Niagara Archives.

View of the Old Fort, from the lamp level of the Lighthouse, c. 1900.

Old Fort Niagara Archives.

ever, the post would be functioning as a training base for volunteers recruited for service in the Philippine Islands. These new possessions of the United States had been taken from Spain in 1898. Between 1899 and 1901, however, a major military effort was required to quell a rebellion of Filipinos seeking independence. The 42nd Regiment of United States Volunteers trained for this service at Fort Niagara in the fall of 1899.

Fort Niagara also served as a training base during the First World War. Many wooden "temporary" buildings were constructed to house large numbers of officers who attended training camps at the post. The post-war years saw a return to peaceful garrison life for a battalion of regular infantry. The unit most often associated with Fort Niagara during this time was the 28th Regiment, United States Infantry. Fort Niagara perhaps typified the lean but quiet days of the "Old Army." New equipment was scarce and the number of troops was relatively small, but the post was a showplace of military neatness.

During these years the historic buildings of Old Fort Niagara continued to decay. Most were used for storage, though civilian employees of the Army lived in the French Castle until about 1915. By the early 1920's, however, the Old Fort was in danger of being lost. The buildings were falling apart, and Lake Ontario had undermined the stone seawall. Concern grew among local citizens who were well aware of the fort's importance to the history of the Niagara Frontier. In 1927, these people formed the Old Fort Niagara Association with the goal

of restoring the fort as a museum. The Association obtained the cooperation and financial assistance of the Army, and solicited private donations. Restoration of the French Castle began in 1927, and was completed two years later. Between 1929 and 1932 the other structures were repaired and restored to their eighteenth century appearances. Additional work was completed by 1934. The Old Fort has been operated as a historic site museum since that time.

New Fort Niagara continued as an active post throughout this time. The garrison maintained close ties with the local populace. Colonel Charles Morrow, commander from 1930 to 1935, channeled much of the troops' energy into the restoration of the Old Fort. Dress parades, band concerts and other public events were also a regular part of garrison routine. The chief duties were still military, however, and training was a major part of daily activities.

The end of this quiet but colorful period came in 1940, when the 28th Infantry was transferred to South Carolina. Fort Niagara, by now

too small to be useful as a training ground for modern war, was converted into an induction center. Thousands of Western New Yorkers had their first taste of army life in the brick barracks of Fort Niagara. In 1944, part of the military post was fenced and set aside for use as a prisoner of war camp. German soldiers captured in North Africa, many of them members of General Erwin Rommel's famous Afrika Korps, were held at the post. They spent the next two years working under guard on local farms. The camp was closed in 1946.

The conclusion of the Second World War should also have spelled the end of the active post at Fort Niagara. All military units were withdrawn in 1945, and the buildings were used briefly as emergency housing for returning veterans. The intention was to convert the area to a New York State Park, however, to complement the museum in the Old Fort. This was delayed by the Korean War when the Army reactivated the post. It was used for a variety of purposes over the next decade. Newly developed air defense missiles were then being installed

The French Castle in use as married soldiers' quarters, July 1, 1874.

Restoration work on the Castle, by War Department employed workers.

Maj. Alfred G. Adams, Corps of Engineers, supervised.

Restoration well in progress, early 1930's.

Both photos: Old Fort Niagara Archives.

**Thor Borresen (left),
Maj. Alfred G. Adams, C.E. (right),
and "Scott," June 13, 1929.**

**Colonel Charles Morrow,
28th Infantry Regiment, US Army,
championed restoration work.**

to protect the hydroelectric plants and industries of the Niagara Frontier. Fort Niagara provided barracks and headquarters facilities. The end finally came in 1963. At that time, the United States Army formally ceded the property to the State of New York, and the last regular soldiers marched off the post. The long military history of traditional army troops at Fort Niagara — be they French, British or American — had finally ended.

Today, surviving walls and buildings of Old Fort Niagara are maintained by the Old Fort Niagara Association, Inc., a not-for-profit educational organization, under license from the New York State Office of Parks, Recreation and Historic Preservation. The Old Fort is a Registered National Historic Landmark. Most of the nineteenth and twentieth century buildings of New Fort Niagara were removed in 1965 and 1966 to clear the area for a recreational park. A few survivors may still be seen today in the area known as Fort Niagara State Park. A United States Coast Guard Station is the only remaining military facility on a site whose history has spanned three hundred years.

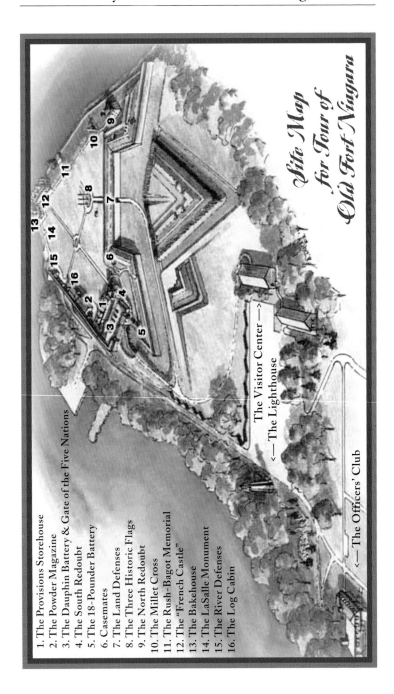

Site Map for Tour of Old Fort Niagara

The Visitor Center —>
<— The Lighthouse
<— The Officers' Club

1. The Provisions Storehouse
2. The Powder Magazine
3. The Dauphin Battery & Gate of the Five Nations
4. The South Redoubt
5. The 18-Pounder Battery
6. Casemates
7. The Land Defenses
8. The Three Historic Flags
9. The North Redoubt
10. The Millet Cross
11. The Rush–Bagot Memorial
12. The "French Castle"
13. The Bakehouse
14. The LaSalle Monument
15. The River Defenses
16. The Log Cabin

Old Fort Niagara: a Tour of the Historic Site

(Please refer to site map on pages 52)

The long and complex history of Old Fort Niagara is well represented by the architecture which may be seen at the site. Each of the nations which held the post replaced or added to the fortifications and buildings, to meet their particular needs. In the years between the late seventeenth century and the Civil War, hundreds of different structures stood within the walls. Those which remain represent the most durable construction, and give some idea of how much the fort changed through its history.

From 1726 until 1872, Fort Niagara was considered a defensible fortified place. By the end of the Civil War, however, the old walls were acknowledged to be obsolete. The focus of military activity and construction then shifted to the area east of the fortifications. After 1872, Old Fort Niagara was viewed largely as a historical curiosity, and the Army utilized the old buildings primarily for storage. They were thus preserved, until local efforts culminated in their restoration between 1927 and 1934.

Today, Old Fort Niagara contains one of the finest collections of eighteenth century military architecture in North America. The buildings, with the exception of the Log Cabin and the present Gatehouse, were constructed between 1726 and 1771. The shape of the fort even dates to the 1750's, although the fortifications represent many stages of development from the following century. For purposes of this tour, the major features of Old Fort Niagara are numbered and keyed to a site map. Follow the numbers for the most comprehensive visit.

1. THE PROVISIONS STOREHOUSE (1762): This long stone building was erected by the British in 1762, on the site of an earlier French warehouse. The Provisions Storehouse was designed to ease the problems of supplying military posts on the Great Lakes. Fort Niagara was well situated to serve as the main depot for provisions. Food intended for the western garrisons at Detroit and Michilimackinac was stored in this building until it could be moved across the Niagara

View (back) of the 1762 Provisions Storehouse .

Old Fort Niagara Archives.

Portage to Lake Erie. The Provisions Storehouse also contained supplies for the garrison of Fort Niagara.

British soldiers of the eighteenth century were provided with a basic ration which they supplemented with vegetables grown in their own gardens, or wild foods bartered from the Indians. The ration staples consisted of flour, salted meat (usually pork), butter, dried peas, and rice. Most of this food was produced in the British Isles, packaged in heavy wooden casks and shipped to North America. Dried and salted foods could be preserved for long periods. This was necessary at a time when it could easily take two years to transport a barrel of provisions to Niagara, and another to move it as far west as Michigan.

Within this storehouse, the garrison Commissary received and issued provisions, while his cooper (barrel maker) repaired damaged casks. Constant loading and unloading during the long journey from Europe was hard on the provisions containers. In addition to such unavoidable damage, the Commissary frequently discovered that the boatmen had drained the brine from barrels of salt pork. This was done to lighten their load during the numerous portages along the St. Lawrence River. Upon reaching Lake Ontario, they refilled the casks with fresh water so no difference in weight would be detected. The meat, of course, quickly spoiled from a lack of "pickle." As much as thirty percent of the provisions which reached Niagara during the 1760's was so damaged as to be inedible!

Old Fort Niagara Archives.

1757 French Powder Magazine; entry porch added by British c. 1771.

The Provisions Storehouse, as originally constructed, was much different than it is today. The ground floor walls were built of stone, and they have survived. However, the building originally had a wooden second story with a loft. This was removed sometime during the early nineteenth century. The capacity of the Provisions Storehouse was immense. Seven thousand barrels of provisions, each about the size of a 55 gallon drum and weighing over two hundred pounds, could be stored on its three levels. The casks were hoisted to the upper floors by means of pulleys and trap doors. There was also a cellar for the storage of butter.

By the time of the War of 1812, the great capacity of the Provisions Storehouse was no longer needed. After the upper story was removed, the building served the United States Army as a combination Quartermaster's and Ordnance Storehouse. A shortage of housing at the post following the Civil War necessitated conversion of the old building to barracks and quarters for laundresses. It was later used briefly as a stable. By the 1920's, the Provisions Storehouse was in ruins. It was restored to its present appearance in 1930.

2. THE POWDER MAGAZINE (1757): This massive structure is one of two surviving French buildings in Old Fort Niagara. It was erected in 1757 for the storage of gunpowder. More spacious than most garrison magazines in New France, this building was intended to

Top of the massive stone arch, outer ceiling, 1757 Powder Magazine.

Old Fort Niagara Archives.

contain the large quantities of explosives needed to support French military operations in the Ohio Valley.

The early French garrisons of Fort Niagara were small and did not require great amounts of gunpowder. Their storage needs were satisfied by a small magazine on the ground floor of the "French Castle" (Point 12). When the fortifications were expanded between 1755 and 1757, a larger magazine became necessary. The new building was completed by the summer of 1757, and demonstrated its sturdiness during the siege of 1759.

The Magazine was carefully designed to withstand hostile bombardment. Its four foot thick walls were proof against most cannon balls. The ceiling was formed by a heavy stone arch. This barrier was further reinforced against falling mortar bombs by a thick layer of earth and rubble between the arch and the roof.

The French Powder Magazine provided the main storage for explosives for the remainder of Old Fort Niagara's active service. Ammunition was kept in the building as late as the First World War. The structure was altered only slightly during its long use. Prior to the American Revolution, the British added the stone porch around the single doorway, and buttressed the outer walls. During the early 1840's, the buttresses were removed, and ventilation was improved by the installation of windows at the ends, and a baffled slit in each corner.

During the eighteenth century, the interior of the Powder Magazine was filled with wooden racks supporting hundreds of kegs of gunpowder. These extended to the ceiling, and the building could easily contain fifty tons of explosives. Floor and walls were sheathed with wooden plank in an effort to protect the powder from moisture. No iron fittings were used, however, since they could cause a fatal spark. The present floor dates to the nineteenth century.

The only deviation from this building's long use as a powder magazine occurred during the Morgan Incident of 1826. William Morgan had become disillusioned with the practice of Freemasonry, and published a booklet exposing its secrets. One faction among Western New York's Masons reacted violently. They kidnapped Morgan and carried him to the Niagara Frontier. Fort Niagara had been abandoned by the United States Army earlier in the year, so the Magazine and the fort were unoccupied. The lone caretaker was himself a Mason, and cooperated in the affair. Morgan was confined in the Magazine, but soon disappeared, never to be seen again. No one has ever conclusively explained his fate. The Masons were loudly accused of murder, but no charges were proven. They, in turn, maintained that Morgan had left the country. Whatever his fate, the "Morgan Incident" sparked much anti-Masonic feeling in New York and across the country.

3. THE DAUPHIN BATTERY AND GATE OF THE FIVE NATIONS (1756): By the end of 1756, Fort Niagara had been transformed by the French from a small wooden stockade into a massive earthwork fortress covering twelve acres. The new land side walls required a protected entrance for friendly troops and Indians. A gate was established in a sheltered corner of the South Bastion. It was well shielded from the east or land side of the fort. The French christened the gate "Porte des Cinq Nations," or Gate of the Five Nations, to honor the original five nations of the Iroquois Indians.

Access to the new gateway was impeded by the ditch which surrounded the entire land side of the fort. Friendly forces could cross this barrier by means of a wooden bridge and drawbridge. In time of attack the drawbridge could be raised, and the stationary bridge burned to make an attack more difficult.

The Gate of the Five Nations was further guarded by a battery of heavy guns located just north of the entrance. The weapons sited here could sweep the entrance with grapeshot and canister. The guns also pointed up the Niagara River toward the Falls to cover the road along the river. Today, as then, the Niagara Escarpment is visible six miles upstream at Lewiston. On clear days, the mist rising above Niagara Falls, nearly fifteen miles to the south, is sometimes visible.

Old Fort Niagara Archives.

Gate of the Five Nations *(Porte des Cinq Nations)*.

The Gate of the Five Nations was the main entrance to Fort Niagara until about 1805. At that time it was filled in and the drawbridge removed. Access to the fort was thereafter through a gateway on the river side near the existing Postern Gate (see Point 15). The Gate of the Five Nations, with its stone head house, was reconstructed in 1930.

4. THE SOUTH REDOUBT (1770): The Gate of the Five Nations originally opened directly into the interior of Fort Niagara. The only fortification behind the gate was a wooden guardhouse located on the right, as one entered. By the late 1760's, however, the British garrison required a more substantial guard post at this point. A variety of plans culminated, in 1770, with construction of the South Redoubt. A similar building, the North Redoubt, was begun at the same time and completed in 1771.

Old Fort Niagara Archives.

The 1756 Dauphin Battery (above), restored in 1931, was named in honor of the eldest son of King Louis XV, Prince Louis (right), *dauphin de France*, heir apparent to the French throne, and future Louis XVI.

The need for these imposing structures was created by the continued deterioration of the fortifications of Fort Niagara. Once the French regime had been driven from America in 1760, the British garrison had little to fear from a European enemy. The most likely adversaries were the Indians, and they had no artillery. Heavy earthwork walls were not needed to resist their assaults, so the fortifications of Niagara were allowed to crumble. The only reinforcement of the defenses was a wooden stockade constructed around the "Castle" (Point 12) in 1768.

With the earthen walls and ditches in ruins, the British relied on the new stockade for security from a surprise attack. This defense was soon considered inadequate, and plans for advanced blockhouses or redoubts were studied. These were to be constructed on or just inside the ruined earthworks, to provide advance guard posts and a crossfire against anyone assaulting the stockaded Castle.

Plans for two stone redoubts were completed by 1770, and work began that summer. One building was situated within each of the two bastions of the land side defenses. The possibility of reconstructing the

The South Redoubt (1770). The heaviest fighting inside the Fort during the War of 1812 took place here on December 19, 1813.

Old Fort Niagara Archives.

earthworks had not been discarded, however, and the new redoubts were designed to allow cannon on their upper floors to cover the walls.

The South Redoubt was the first of the two new buildings to be completed. Its ground floor was pierced by a passageway equipped with two sets of heavy gates. The building thus provided a secondary defense for the main entrance. The floor above was equipped as a guard room for twenty men. A "guard" was formed from the garrison each day, and its members served for the next twenty-four hours. These men provided the sentries, and were always prepared to resist a surprise attack. The guard room was their base of operations. Here the soldiers were allowed to relax while not actually on sentry duty, though they were always fully clothed and prepared to repel an attack. The third level of the South Redoubt provided a sturdy gun platform for light artillery, usually six-pounders, to cover the east front of Fort Niagara.

The South Redoubt protected the main entrance until about 1805 when the Gate of the Five Nations was removed. The building continued in use as a guardhouse during the War of 1812. In the fall of 1812 the roof was removed to allow the Redoubt to serve more efficiently as a gun platform. The gunners' target, Fort George, may be seen about 1,200 yards upstream on the Canadian shore. During the surprise British assault of December 19, 1813, the attackers encountered stiff resistance from sixty-five American soldiers stationed in the South Redoubt. The British finally smashed open the door, fought their way up two flights of stairs and forced the defenders to capitulate.

The South Redoubt underwent many changes during the nineteenth century. In the 1840's, the arched gateways were walled in, and a powder magazine was constructed on the ground floor. In its later years, the building served quietly as a provisions storehouse. It was restored to its eighteenth century appearance in 1929.

5. 18-POUNDER BATTERY (1843): On several occasions during the War of 1812 the garrison of Fort Niagara exchanged furious artillery fire with Fort George. The heaviest American guns were mounted on the river side of the South Bastion. From this spot the view is directly toward Fort George, visible across the river above the houses of Niagara-on-the-Lake.

When the defenses of Fort Niagara were modernized between 1839 and 1843 the river side of the post received the most attention. Much of the work was defensive in nature and involved the construction of new walls. Improvements were also made to the offensive capabilities of the fort. New emplacements for heavy cannon were established to face Canada. Most of these positions were intended to mount eighteen-pounder cannon, so called because of the weight of shot they fired. Fort Niagara's eighteen-pounders were to be mounted "en barbette" (firing over the wall) on seacoast style gun carriages. This allowed them a considerable field of fire, though the crews were exposed to the enemy. The front of each carriage was set on a pintle with the rear supported on wheels. These ran on semicircular iron rails for rapid traversing. Altogether nine positions for eighteen-pounders were planned for the river side of Fort Niagara. Three were located on the South Bastion.

Like so many nineteenth century fortification projects, Fort Niagara's 1839-1843 improvements were never completed. Although the walls were finished, only a few guns were ever mounted. By 1872 these were obsolete and the fortifications largely abandoned.

From the 18-Pounder Battery it is possible to obtain a good view up the Niagara River toward the village of Youngstown, New York, one mile distant. The area between the village and the fort was the Military Reserve, first laid out by the British in 1760 to prevent civilian encroachment on the fort. Following the Civil War, the Reserve was developed with a complex of barracks and officers' quarters. By the 1870's, this area, "New" Fort Niagara, was the center of military activities. United States troops occupied the New Fort until 1963. Also visible from this point is the Fort Niagara Lighthouse, constructed in 1871. The beacon at the top of the tower guided vessels into the Niagara River until 1993, when a new system was installed by the Coast Guard.

6. CASEMATES (1872): The brick facing along the length of the Land Defenses of Fort Niagara was constructed during the Civil War era. Important features of these fortifications were a pair of subterranean galleries from which muskets and cannon could be fired at anyone approaching the main walls. These "casemates" were the result of a final attempt to maintain Fort Niagara as an effective fortification.

A casemate gallery is located in each of the bastions of Fort Niagara. The largest part of these underground shelters was devoted to positions for four 24-pounder howitzers. Four of these short, heavy guns were to have been mounted in each gallery. The weapons were termed "flanking howitzers" because they were designed to flank the walls with anti-personnel ammunition. Each charge was composed of many small projectiles which could devastate columns of enemy infantry once they entered the ditch. Although the two galleries face each other, the grapeshot and canister from their guns would not cause serious damage to the opposite wall. The fields of fire of the two galleries interlocked to cover every part of the ditch. Ventilators near the ceiling were designed to dissipate the tremendous amounts of smoke created by the discharge of black powder weapons.

Farther along the gallery are positions from which infantrymen could discharge their muskets at the enemy through long loopholes. At the end of the gallery is a small powder magazine.

By the time the casemate galleries had been completed, their usefulness was in doubt. The flanking howitzers were never mounted.

7. THE LAND DEFENSES (1755-1872): The massive walls which form the east or land side of Fort Niagara have undergone many changes. Surprisingly, the original eighteenth century lines of these

View of the South Casemate Gallery (1872). Both North and South Casemates contain four 24-pounder flanking howitzers, dedicated powder magines, vent shafts, and individual firing positions for musket or riflemen.

Old Fort Niagara Archives.

fortifications have been preserved. Most of the changes have been superficial, and much remains from the original construction of the 1750's. The Land Defenses were designed by Captain Pierre Pouchot, an officer in the French Regiment of Bearn. Pouchot used great economy in converting Fort Niagara from a simple stockade to a proper eighteenth century fortification. He designed the walls to connect the lake and the river, effectively cutting off and securing the end of the peninsula. The main fortifications faced the land, the side from which a British attack was most likely to come.

The Land Defenses of Fort Niagara comprise a thick earthen wall fronted by a deep dry ditch or "fosse." The wall was further shielded by detached outworks and a sloping "glacis." The effect was to make the fortifications virtually invisible to the artillerymen of an attacking force. The result can best be seen by looking at the fort from the parking lot. Only the very top of the wall is visible across the sloping glacis. And yet, attacking soldiers would be confronted by a wide and deep ditch when they reached the top of the glacis.

The main lines of the Land Defenses consist of a pair of bastions (actually "half" bastions) connected by a "curtain" or straight wall. The curtain is pierced by a gateway known as a "sally port." During the

View across the top of the Scarp Walls, from the top deck of the South Redoubt. The central "Curtain Wall" connects two bastions, and is pierced by the Sally Port gateway.

Photo, courtesy of Lawrence Fortunato.

summer months, the sally port provides access to the outer defenses. Across the ditch, opposite the curtain, is a large triangular fortification known as a "ravelin." Its function was to shield the curtain and sally port from direct cannon fire. On either side of the ravelin were smaller triangular fortifications known as "lunettes." Only the lunette on the river side of the ravelin exists today. In advance of all the outworks was a "covered way," a sheltered path where the defenders could walk in safety and fire at the enemy across the glacis.

These lines have been superficially altered a number of times. The original walls were constructed of earth faced with sod to prevent erosion. A palisade of wooden pickets was placed about halfway up the wall to impede attacking infantry. The original wall construction was much like that visible on the ravelin or the walls on either side of the Gate of the Five Nations.

Sometime after the American Revolution, the land side walls were faced with heavy plank. This was an attempt to prevent erosion of the walls, which had been a chronic problem with the sod facing. Replanking of the earthworks was a major part of the repairs from 1839 to 1843.

The final alteration to the land defenses of Fort Niagara occurred between 1863 and 1872. The planking was removed and replaced by a revetment of poured concrete faced with red brick. The casemate gal-

Old Fort Niagara Archives.

leries (Point 6) were installed as part of this design. The new walls were intended to resist mid-nineteenth century artillery, but technological advances were too rapid. The defenses were obsolete by the time of their completion.

8. THE THREE HISTORICAL FLAGS: In the center of the fort are three flagpoles which daily fly the historical colors of the three nations which have occupied Old Fort Niagara. This tradition dates to the early 1930's when restoration of the Fort was completed. The flags are symbolic of three hundred years of military activity at the mouth of the Niagara River. Earliest of the banners is the flag of France. From the establishment of a permanent fort at Niagara in 1726, until its capture by the British in 1759, this white flag flew above the walls. Although its appearance is today associated with a sign of surrender, flags were not so standardized in the eighteenth century. There were a variety of French banners. That of the Marine Department, the agency responsible for France's navy and colonies, was white. This flag was displayed on French warships and colonial fortifications around the globe.

The British Union Jack was raised above the walls of Fort Niagara in 1759, and remained until 1796. The version flown in the Fort today, was in use until 1801. It displays the red cross of St. George and the white X-shaped cross of St. Andrew representing England and Scotland respectively. The modern Union Jack includes the red X-shaped cross of St. Patrick which was added to the flag in 1801, following union with Ireland. That version of the British flag flew over Fort Niagara briefly from December, 1813, to May, 1815. The third flag symbolizes the United States occupation of Fort Niagara. Although many different versions of the Stars and Stripes have flown over the walls, the 15 stars and stripes banner displayed today, was in use from 1794 to 1818. A flag of this design flying over Fort McHenry during a British bombardment in 1814, inspired Francis Scott Key to compose the lyrics to what would become the U.S. National Anthem.

9. THE NORTH REDOUBT (1771): Like the similar South Redoubt, this building was designed to support light artillery on its second floor, while a guard of twenty men could be sheltered on the first floor. The chief difference between the two structures is the ground floor. While the South Redoubt is pierced by a gateway, the North Redoubt has only a small door on the west facade. Its ground floor interior originally included a small powder magazine.

Construction of the North Redoubt commenced during 1770. A shortage of laborers delayed completion until 1771, however. The building otherwise followed much the same history as the South Redoubt. Its roof was removed during the War of 1812 and replaced after the conflict. Alterations, including a new ground floor powder magazine, were made in the 1840's. By the end of the nineteenth century, the old structure was serving the United States Army as a storehouse for Engineer, Ordnance and Signal Corps equipment. Restoration was accomplished in 1930.

Old Fort Niagara Archives.

The North Redoubt, begun in 1770 with its mate, was not completed until 1771. The ground floor differs greatly from the South's.

Fort Niagara's pair of stone redoubts are unique in North America. They were designed by British engineers in New York, and the plans were sent to Niagara for execution. Lieutenant John Montresor probably designed both buildings. Construction, however, was under the supervision of the post engineer, Lieutenant Francis Pfister. Limestone for the walls was obtained from a quarry at the Lower Landing, six miles up the river. This back breaking labor was performed by soldiers from the garrison who then moved the stone down the river to Fort Niagara in scows. Civilian masons from New York were contracted to erect the walls.

Although the redoubts were severely functional buildings, their designer incorporated two very different architectural styles popular in eighteenth century Britain. The stone tower of each displays elements of Classical Greek and Roman architecture: temple fronts, pediments, arched windows and doors, and a belt course of stone near the parapet. The roofs, however, have the flaring eaves of a Chinese pagoda. Chinese and Classical styles were both very popular in European architecture, design and decorative arts of the mid-eighteenth century.

The Father Millet Cross (1926) was once, a full United States National Monument, and had the added distinction of being the smallest such designee. Annual religious pilgrimages to the site have been conducted since 1926, by the Knights of Columbus.

10. THE MILLET CROSS (1926): One of the earliest efforts to erect a monument to the history of Old Fort Niagara occurred in 1926. A project of the Knights of Columbus, the Millet Cross overlooks Lake Ontario, and commemorates an event which occurred in the seventeenth century. The parcel for the Father Millet Cross was set aside by Presidential proclamation on September 5, 1925, and declared a National Monument (under the jurisdiction of the War Department) at the same time, even though the final structure was not yet created. The bronze cross was erected in 1926, and the Knights have held an annual pilgrimage to site every year since. The Cross, which had the distinction of being the smallest U.S. National Monument, was transferred to the jurisdiction of the National Park Service in 1933. A series of restructurings, approved by Congress, resulted in abolishment of the federal designation on September 7, 1949, at which time the Cross and its 0.0074 acre plot of land were transferred to the State of New York.

Following the establishment of Fort Denonville by the French in the summer of 1687, a garrison was left for the winter. Isolated from the nearest friendly post by the elements and hostile Iroquois Indians, the soldiers slowly starved, sickened and died. By spring, only twelve of the original one hundred remained alive. Their lives were saved by the arrival of a relief force on Good Friday, 1688.

Accompanying the French relief force was Father Pierre Millet, a Jesuit noted missionary priest. At Millet's orders, the troops erected a tall oak cross in the center of the fort. On it was carved the abbreviated Latin inscription "Regn. Vinc. Imp. Chrs." ("Regnat, Vincit, Imperat, Christus" – "Christ Reigneth, Conquereth, Ruleth"). Under this cross, the men sang a "Te Deum," and Millet offered a Mass of thanksgiving for the survival of the fortunate few members of the unlucky garrison.

The actual location of Fort Denonville is unknown, other than that it was somewhere within the bounds of Fort Niagara. Most accounts indicate that the site of the stockade and Millet's cross was that now occupied by the French Castle (Point 12).

11. THE RUSH-BAGOT MEMORIAL (1934): Old Fort Niagara stands on the edge of an international boundary. Canada is visible across the Niagara River to the west as well as to the north across Lake Ontario. Although this border is accurately known as the longest unfortified international boundary in the world, such has not always been the case. Fort Niagara was only one of a number of fortifications maintained along the northern margin of the United States in the late eighteenth and nineteenth centuries. British posts faced the Americans across the intervening waters of the Great Lakes, and border tensions were often high.

The worst period of relations came between 1812 and 1815 when United States troops clashed with British and Canadian forces along the northern borders. Fort Niagara was heavily involved in the War of 1812. Fort George and Fort Mississauga, still visible across the river, also date to that traumatic period. In addition to fortifications, numerous warships were launched on the Great Lakes as both sides sought to

Monument photos: Courtesy, Lawrence Fortunato.

control the waterways. This naval arms race had, by the end of the war, placed the most powerful warships of the British and United States navies on Lake Ontario. Fortunately, the post-war years witnessed genuine efforts to reduce tensions between the two countries.

In 1817, the United States and Great Britain signed the Rush-Bagot Agreement (formally ratified as a treaty by the United States on April 28, 1818, and by Great Britain on October 2, 1818). It placed strict limits on naval armaments on the waters of the Great Lakes. The treaty is still in effect, and even influences Coast Guard armaments and good-will cruises by modern United States and Canadian warships.

The Rush-Bagot Memorial at Old Fort Niagara was completed and dedicated in 1934. It honors the treaty and its two principal negotiators, Richard Rush and Sir Charles Bagot, who gave their names to the accord. The true monument to their success is today's 4000 mile unfortified United States-Canadian border.

In addition to its commemorative significance, the memorial is also a tomb. During the restoration of Old Fort Niagara from 1926 to 1934, several minor archeological excavations took place. During this work, skeletal remains were encountered. Some of the burials were discovered a mere 11 inches below the surface. When the Rush-Bagot Monument was constructed, a suitable crypt was incorporated into the center platform of the memorial, and all the remains were reinterred there in a sealed aluminum container. The exact location is marked by an engraved capstone.

The stonework of the Rush-Bagot Memorial is supported by the most massive and least noticeable part of the Fort Niagara defenses. A stone seawall stretching from the North Redoubt to the French Castle protected the fort not from the ravages of cannon fire but from the encroachment of Lake Ontario. Erosion had plagued Fort Niagara since the 1720's. When the French Castle was constructed in 1726, it stood about two hundred feet from the edge of Lake Ontario. The seawall, erected between 1839 and 1843, halted the lake only fifteen feet from the historic building.

In clear weather, the skyline of Toronto, Ontario, Canada, is visible from the Rush-Bagot Memorial. The metropolis is twenty-seven miles across Lake Ontario.

12. THE FRENCH CASTLE (1726): Oldest and largest of the buildings of Fort Niagara is the "French Castle." This unique and durable structure has guarded the entrance of the Niagara River for more than 280 years. It is the oldest building in North America between the Appalachian Mountains and the Mississippi River, and on the Great Lakes.

The Castle was the nucleus of the fort established by the French in 1726. Construction began that summer, and was nearly finished by the end of the year. It was completed in 1727. Fort Niagara and its "Castle" were the result of years of persuasion and negotiation by French agents to the Iroquois, who finally agreed to a French post at Niagara, in Seneca territory, providing that it not be a regular fortification. The French seemed to oblige by constructing a stone "House of Peace" for trading, enclosed by a simple wooden stockade. Reality, was a different story.

The building was more than just a trading house, however. Its stone walls were proof against muskets and arrows. Many features were also designed into the house to ensure that its garrison could successfully resist an attack by Iroquois warriors or British raiders. The building was intended to shelter all the needs for a garrison of sixty men. Quarters, storehouses, a powder magazine and even a well were located within its walls. The Senecas realized the cunning deception too late to stop it.

The French Castle was used for its original purpose for only the first twenty years of its long history. By the late 1740's, the stockade had been enlarged to include additional barracks, storehouses and a bakery. Ten years later, the fort was increased to its present size, and more buildings were erected. The stone house was no longer the only structure of the post. As many of its functions were assumed by specialized buildings, the Castle was used increasingly for officers' quarters. Following

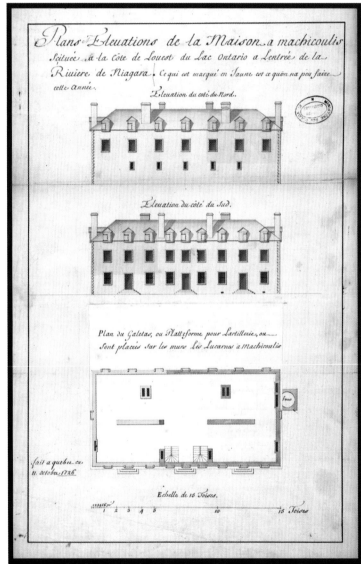

Original 1726 plans for the *maison a machicoulis* (machicolated house) at Niagara, drawn by New France's legendary engineer, Gaspard Chaussegros de Lery (the elder). He produced a master sheet showing the exterior views and the attic plan, then attached flip-up floor plans for the other two levels (page 73). The red shows structural items completed in 1726; the yellow, unfinished.

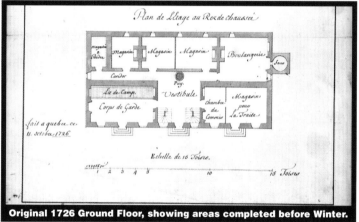

Original 1726 Ground Floor, showing areas completed before Winter.

Original 1726 First Floor, showing progress made before Winter.

their capture of Fort Niagara, the British continued to employ the "large stone house" for officers' apartments. They also began to alter the building to make it more comfortable. Some large rooms were divided. Chimneys were even moved in order to provide apartments for the garrison officers. In 1765, the exterior was plastered and a porch was built around the entrance. Although the last porch was removed about 1920, much of the exterior plaster was still in place.

After 1796, the United States Army utilized the Castle as officers' quarters and storerooms. This continued, with a few interruptions, until the late nineteenth century. After that time, the apartments were occupied by civilian contractors working on the post. The last residents departed about 1915.

By 1925, the historic old building, popular symbol of the French occupation of the Niagara Frontier, was in a sadly deteriorated condition. The Castle had long been recognized as an important historic relic, however, and local residents became alarmed that it might be lost forever. Their concern stimulated efforts to preserve Fort Niagara and led, in 1927, to the formation of the Old Fort Niagara Association. Restoration of the Castle began in 1927, and was completed two years later.

The intention of the restoration was to return the French Castle to its appearance of 1726-1727. The original, highly detailed plans were discovered in the French Archives. These served as the guide for the restoration. Unfortunately, much evidence of the later alterations was indiscriminately removed. The stone walls of the Castle are largely original, however, as are a few wooden beams and other elements of the interior. The rooms were restored to reflect their use in 1727.

• GROUND FLOOR OF THE CASTLE

Visitors enter the French Castle through one of three doors on the ground floor. The middle door provided the main entrance during the eighteenth century. It opened on a central vestibule connecting with all other parts of the ground floor. Two stairways lead to the first floor, and the original well is located opposite the main door. This vestibule and the one directly above it were the gathering places in the original building. The interior of the Castle was, in fact, laid out similarly to the ground plan of a fort. Barracks and storerooms clustered around the vestibules, much as buildings were situated around the parade ground of a fortress. Here, the soldiers could assemble for inspection or to pre-

The Winter Trade by Robert Griffing

pare for duty. The well provided a protected source of drinking water in the event of a siege.

The old well is probably one of the best known features of the French Castle. An 1839 guidebook to the Niagara Falls area, first recounted the story of the headless ghost of a French officer who is said to inhabit the building. On nights when the moon is full, the story continued, he had been observed sitting on the curb of the well. This story has been heavily embroidered over the years, and remains one of the most popular ghost stories of Western New York. No versions of the tale predating 1839 have yet been discovered.

The large size of the vestibule is made possible by a stone arch above the well. The massive construction of the French Castle employed interior partitions of stone which served as load-bearing walls. This strengthened the building and helped support the immense weight of stone flooring on the upper levels. To provide a room of this size, it was necessary to carry the weight of the longitudinal wall across the open space with an arch. A similar structure may also be seen above the first floor vestibule. Both arches lack large central keystones, relying instead on several smaller stones placed at intervals along their lengths.

Two rooms open directly off the ground floor vestibule. To the right is the Trade Room which was an important feature of the Castle in its earliest days. Originally divided by a wooden partition, this area provided storage for trade goods and furs, and quarters for the trade clerk or "commis."

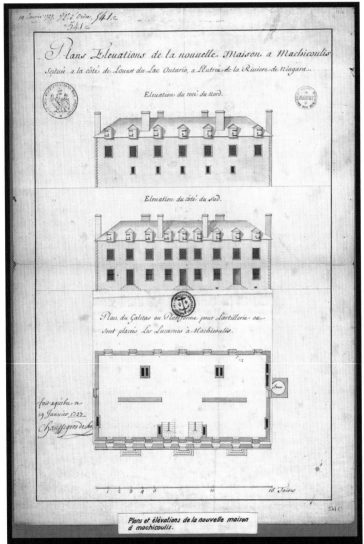

**Original 1727 copy of the 1726 plans for the *maison a machicoulis*
(machicolated house) at Niagara, drawn by Gaspard Chaussegros de
Lery (the elder). As with the 1726 report plans (Pages 72 - 73), he
produced a master sheet showing the exterior views and the attic,
then attached flip-up floor plans for the other two levels
(page 77). The red shows that all structural items were now
complete, and the building was fully usable as planned.**

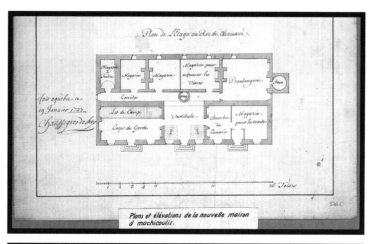

Plans et élévations de la nouvelle maison à machicoulis.

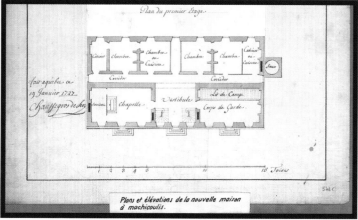

Plans et élévations de la nouvelle maison à machicoulis.

A monopoly on the local fur trade was a lucrative perquisite of the commandant of a frontier military post in New France. Trading activities were controlled by this officer. From his profits, he reserved shares for the Governor of the colony and the King. Although trade continued at Fort Niagara throughout the French period, the post gradually lost its importance, as the nearby population of fur-bearing animals was destroyed. When the fort was enlarged in the 1740's, the Trade Room was converted for other purposes. By the 1760's, its exterior door had been converted to a window. The room today represents a typical trading post where Indians bartered furs for European manufactured goods. By 1927, the French Castle and the Bakehouse were in derelict condition.

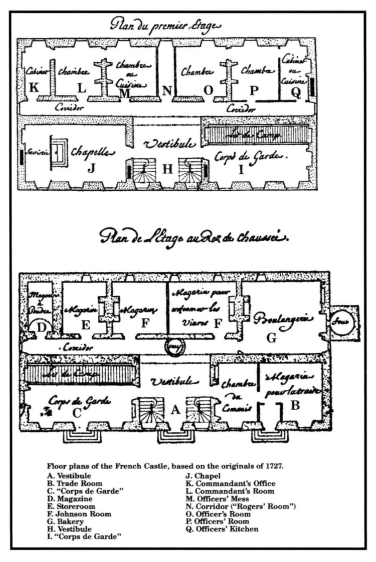

Floor plans of the French Castle, based on the originals of 1727.

A. Vestibule
B. Trade Room
C. "Corps de Garde"
D. Magazine
E. Storeroom
F. Johnson Room
G. Bakery
H. Vestibule
I. "Corps de Garde"

J. Chapel
K. Commandant's Office
L. Commandant's Room
M. Officers' Mess
N. Corridor ("Rogers' Room")
O. Officer's Room
P. Officers' Room
Q. Officers' Kitchen

At the left of the vestibule is a soldiers' barracks, called a "Corps de Garde" or guardhouse on the original plans. Located adjacent to the main doorway, it might well have served as a guardroom for the entrance to the building. The room also provided living quarters for as many as thirty French enlisted men. The soldiers slept on pallets placed in the long shelf bunk. Meals were prepared in the fireplace and eaten in the room. The barracks was, for the most part, the extent of the private soldier's world when he was not on guard duty, at work, or drilling.

The rear of the vestibule is intersected by a corridor which connects with five more rooms. The rear part of the ground floor provided most of the original French garrison's storage space. The first room on the far left was the powder magazine. With its single door and thick stone ceiling arch, the room is a miniature version of the much larger Powder Magazine constructed in 1757 (Point 2). The new building rendered a magazine in the Castle unnecessary, though small quantities of ammunition were stored here in later years. The British and the Americans occasionally used this room as a "black hole" or solitary confinement cell. One such incident occurred in 1770 when the British imprisoned two Seneca Indians in the old magazine, after they had robbed some traders and mortally wounded a soldier.

The next room on the corridor was originally designed as a general storeroom. At some point in its history, however, it too was used as a cell. The walls are still marked by graffiti believed to date from the eighteenth century. It is visible near the single window, protected by a Plexiglas shield. The room was restored as a cell in 1929.

The central room is one of the largest in the Castle. It reflects the British period of occupation rather than that of the French. This space was originally divided by a wooden partition to create two storerooms. The end nearest the bakery housed provisions. The other chamber was a general storeroom.

Tradition maintains that the British removed the partition and opened up the room to provide an officers' mess and council chamber. The restoration reflects this use. The room is dedicated to the memory of Sir William Johnson, who led British forces at the capture of Fort Niagara. Johnson was best known for his work as Superintendent of Indian Affairs. On two occasions, he used Fort Niagara as a meeting place for huge councils with the Native peoples of the Great Lakes.

The last room on the ground floor corridor (far right) was the bakery. Bread for the garrison was baked here from flour which had been shipped to Fort Niagara from Montreal. About 1745, the bakery in the Castle was replaced by a separate building. The end of the room is distinguished by a single large oven which projects outside the wall. Its back is visible on the east facade of the building.

• FIRST FLOOR OF THE CASTLE

The first floor of the French Castle was used primarily for living quarters. The rear of the building (the lake side) was reserved for officers. French enlisted men bunked on the land side above the entrance door. As on the ground floor, the rooms cluster around a central vestibule.

To the right of the vestibule is a second "Corps de Garde," occupied by soldiers. It is virtually identical to the barracks on the ground floor. Following the British occupation, this room, along with the Trade Room below, was divided in two and equipped with a central chimney to provide more comfortable officers' apartments.

Opening off the left of the vestibule is the Chapel, an important feature of any eighteenth century French garrison. This room was the first permanent house of worship in Western New York. Roman Catholic priests, all Franciscan Récollets, not Jesuits, were stationed at the post periodically as garrison chaplains, but the chapel was fully adorned from its beginning. There was a chaplain present during the siege in 1759, and he performed his duties admirably.

The chapel in the French Castle was in use until 1757, when it was replaced by a separate building located near the three Flag Poles (Point 8). The chapel room was eventually divided by a partition and chimney, and converted to officers' quarters.

A corridor runs across the rear of the first floor vestibule. Seven rooms, mostly officers' apartments of the French period, connect to this corridor. They provided a semi-private area for the more privileged officers within the crowded confines of the French Castle.

The room at the extreme left of the corridor stands above the powder magazine. It is identified as a "cabinet" on the original plans, and was probably an office for the commanding officer and his clerk. The stone floor of this room is the only survivor of the paving which distinguished the building, and greatly reduced the danger of accidental fire. The stone floors of all the other rooms, each supported by a wooden sub-floor, were removed sometime before 1773 and replaced with wooden plank. Because this floor is supported by the stone arch of the powder magazine, however, it was not necessary or expedient to replace it.

Adjoining the "cabinet" is an officer's apartment which was probably home to the French commanders of Fort Niagara. It is typical of the other quarters on the lake side of the first floor. The room was heated by a single fireplace and lighted by a window overlooking

Guard Room Photo: Courtesy, Lawrence Fortunato.

Chapel Photo: Courtesy, Geoffrey Harding.

the water. Additionally, the officers' quarters are linked by connecting doors.

This room is one of the few in the French Castle which can be associated with a specific incident in the history of the fort. During the summer of 1759, these were the quarters of Captain Pierre Pouchot, commanding French forces defending Niagara against a British attack. On July 17, after a week of sleepless nights spent directing the defense, Pouchot retired to his chambers for a rest. Moments later, the British unmasked a new battery located across the Niagara River, and opened fire. The first cannon ball arced across the river, struck the chimney of the commandant's room, pierced the flue, crashed down into the fireplace, and rolled across the floor in front of the astounded Pouchot!

Adjacent to the commandant's room was the officers' mess. The French garrison of Fort Niagara included only three to five officers in the years before the French and Indian War. This was the room where they took their meals and socialized with each other.

At the center of the group of officers' rooms is a small chamber or corridor, the purpose of which is unknown. The room might have provided a convenient spot for a sentry to look over Lake Ontario. It might also have served as a storeroom for the officers' provisions or personal goods. Despite uncertainty as to its original purpose, this small room can also be identified with an incident in the history of Fort Niagara. In 1768, well after the British had gained control of the fort, the commanding officer was instructed to make preparations to confine an important prisoner. Shortly thereafter, Major Robert Rogers arrived in chains from the northern Michigan post of Michilimackinac. Rogers had been a famous British ranger during the French and Indian War. His exploits had made his name a household word in eighteenth century America, and would later provide the basis for the twentieth century historical novel and motion picture "Northwest Passage." It was, in fact, Robert Rogers' search for a Northwest Passage which had landed him in this miserable little room. As Governor of Michilimackinac, he had sent out exploring parties to locate the mythical route to the Orient. Instead of being lauded for his efforts, Rogers was accused of treason for allegedly conspiring with Britain's Spanish and French rivals in the Mississippi Valley. He was arrested and transported in chains to Montreal. During that journey, after traversing the Niagara Portage, Rogers languished for two weeks in the old French Castle. Though later found innocent by a Court Martial, his once promising career was ruined by the scandal.

The last three rooms of the first floor include two officers' apartments, and a kitchen where their meals were prepared. The latter pair of rooms are separated by a partition of wood, rather than stone, because there is no supporting cross wall in the bakery be-

Old Fort Niagara Archives.

low. Wooden partitions will also be found above the "Johnson Room."

• ATTIC OF THE CASTLE

The second floor, or attic, comprises a single large room. The day to day use of this huge space is unknown. It was probably employed only for storage, since it was unheated. In the event of an attack, however, the second floor would have played a very important role in the defense of Fort Niagara. The dormers projected from the roof to slightly overhang the facades of the building. This allowed defenders armed with muskets or swivel guns to fire down on the enemy without exposing themselves to return fire. It was this feature which gave the Castle its French name. Gaspard Chaussegros de Lery, the designer of the structure, termed it a *"maison a machicoulis"* or "machicolated house." Machicolations were the overhanging galleries on the walls of a medieval castle which allowed defenders to pour boiling liquids on the enemy. Despite this feature, the French never called the building a "castle." It seems to have been the Americans who romantically dubbed it the "French Castle," sometime around the beginning of the nineteenth century.

The attic was used to mount heavy guns only during the War of 1812. In the autumn of 1812, the American garrison stripped the roof from the building, erected an earthen breastwork atop the stone walls, and mounted three heavy guns. This extreme measure was considered necessary to counter British artillery mounted on higher ground across the river at Fort George. Here, on November 21, 1812, a soldier's wife, remembered in history as Fanny Doyle (her real name was apparently Betsy), helped serve a six-pounder cannon during a furious exchange of fire with Fort George. The fort's commander was so impressed by Mrs. Doyle's actions that he mentioned her in his report of the battle. After the War of 1812, the roof was reconstructed. The existing structural timbers date to about 1816, but the exterior design varied until 1927.

The roof of the French Castle also served as the base for two lighthouses. Sometime between 1775 and 1781, the British installed a small cupola on the roof of the Castle. This contained a lantern to guide ships into the mouth of the Niagara River. It was the first lighthouse on the Great Lakes, but was removed about 1804. In 1823 a new light was mounted on an octagonal pedestal erected atop the building. This supported a lens until 1872, when the stone lighthouse outside Old Fort Niagara was placed in service.

13. BAKEHOUSE (1762): This building was one of the busiest places in late eighteenth century Fort Niagara. Here, bread was baked for the soldiers of the British garrisons, and later, their American successors.

The French had been the first to establish a bakery on this site. Sometime around 1745, they abandoned the bakery on the ground floor of the French Castle and erected a wooden building nearby.

The British continued to use the French bakehouse after 1759, but on June 25, 1761, the building took fire and the wooden elements were destroyed. During the summer of 1762, Lieutenant George Demler, post engineer, directed the construction of a new bakehouse. The original French ovens proved to be partially repairable, and these were incorporated into the new building. Careful observation will reveal a "seam" running up each side of the Bakehouse. This marks the division between the ovens and the stone addition of 1762.

The Bakehouse was used by Fort Niagara's British and American garrisons until 1870. At that time a new wooden bakery was constructed hallway between this building and the Log Cabin (Point 16). The historic stone building was in danger of demolition until the garrison of-

Old Fort Niagara Archives.

The Bakehouse. Ovens, c. 1745; Front area, c. 1762.

ficers, inspired perhaps by the United States Centennial of 1876, recommended that it be repaired and converted to an ordnance storehouse. A stone tablet on the exterior near the window marks the successful completion of this project in 1879, an early example of historic preservation for adaptive reuse. The Bakehouse was thereafter used as a storehouse until abandoned in the 1920's, and restored in 1930. The ovens are quite functional, though not used today for safety reasons; the hearths, however, are in active use as part of the Fort's cooking program.

The interior of this building is quite small, though some plans of the fort indicate that it once had a substantial wooden addition on its south end. A single workroom provided space to mix dough, and gave access to the twin ovens. The baking area was constructed of stone, and lined with brick to resist the ravages of fire. Bread was baked by first starting a blaze in the ovens. Smoke escaped through the oven doors, to be drawn up the chimney. Once the ovens had been sufficiently warmed, the coals were raked onto the hearths below the doors. The dough was then inserted, to be baked by the residual heat in the bricks. The single door oven in the French Castle's earlier bakery functioned in the same manner.

Bread was an important part of the diet of every eighteenth century soldier. The ration for a British enlisted man included one pound per day. Like the rest of the provisions, flour was shipped to Niagara from Europe. In times of shortage, wheat milled in North America was sometimes substituted. The British troops knew the difference, however, and complained loudly when forced to consume New York or Canadian flour.

The Hot Shot Furnace, c. 1843, and Battery.

Old Fort Niagara Archives.

14. THE LA SALLE MONUMENT (1934): The first European structure to occupy the site of Fort Niagara was erected in the winter of 1679 by the French explorer Rene-Robert Cavelier, Sieur de La Salle. He christened his tiny stockaded post "Fort Conti," after Louis Armand de Bourbon, Prince of Conti, and used it to support construction of a sailing vessel (the *Griffin*) miles to the north on the Upper Niagara River, for use on Lake Erie and beyond. The buildings were probably located near the site of the French Castle.

La Salle was one of the truly colorful explorers of the New World. In 1934, New York State honored his achievements with this simple plaque.

15. THE RIVER DEFENSES (1839-1843): The designer of Fort Niagara's heavy earthen walls envisioned an attack from the land side. It was from that direction that hostile artillery could be effectively brought to bear during the eighteenth century. Safely tucked behind these earthworks, the lake and river sides of the fort were not vulnerable. They were, therefore, only lightly fortified with wooden pickets.

The situation of Fort Niagara changed dramatically in 1796. The new American garrison faced British guns across the river, and the defenses of Fort Niagara literally faced the wrong way. This caused much difficulty during the War of 1812, but grand plans to rebuild the walls during the post-war years foundered for want of funds. By the 1830's, there were no fortifications of any sort on the river side of Fort Niagara.

Old Fort Niagara Archives.

The Canadian Rebellion of 1837 badly strained relations between the United States and Britain. Fort Mississauga, the brick tower and earthwork visible on the opposite side of the river's mouth, had been constructed in 1814. It was well sited to fire into the unprotected rear of Fort Niagara. This threat was finally countered by the erection of the massive stone River Wall.

Construction began in 1839 under the direction of Captain William D. Fraser of the Corps of Engineers. Three batteries for heavy guns were placed along the length of the wall. These were to mount eighteen-pounders to strike at Fort Mississauga and the Canadian shore. The wall thoroughly masked the interior of Fort Niagara from enemy guns. A stone seawall, topped by a stout wooden stockade, was constructed along the lake side at the same time. The noticeable color difference in the stone of the River Wall was a result of a change in quarries part way through construction. The River Wall stood full height for its entire length until 1889. By that time, undermining by the lake had rendered the north end of the wall unstable, and it was torn down to prevent a collapse. The north section of the wall was partially reconstructed in 1931.

The River Wall included three positions for heavy guns. The first is located adjacent to the Dauphin Battery (Point 3), and was to have

mounted four guns. The second, or "Hot Shot Battery," is located near the middle of the wall. It was sited to allow one gun to aim at Canada, while two others flanked the wall. The third battery, behind the French Castle, was to mount a single cannon aimed at Fort Mississauga. It was partially dismantled in 1889.

At the foot of the Hot Shot Battery stairs is a shot furnace, completed in 1843. This was little more than a coal-fired oven to heat cannon balls. When fired into a wooden ship or building, the heated shot was virtually impossible to extinguish, and would quickly incinerate the target. By the time of its completion, however, this furnace was obsolescent. It was never used.

The final feature of the River Defenses is located about half way along the wall. The Postern Gate served as the main entrance to Fort Niagara from 1839 until 1930. It stands on the site of earlier river gates dating back to the French period. On December 19,1813, a British assaulting party entered Fort Niagara by forcing open a gate on this spot.

16. THE LOG CABIN & TRADING POST (1932): Constructed of solid chestnut logs during the restoration of Old Fort Niagara, this building was intended to represent one of the many wooden structures which stood within the walls during the eighteenth century, and has been interpreted over the years as a blacksmith and farrier's forge, and an artificer's work shop. It occupies the site of an Ordnance Storehouse constructed by the French in 1757, and used by all three occupying nations until about 1805. The building contains a serviceable forge that was used by restoration experts, including the legendary Thor Borresen, who resided there during part of his later years onsite, and worked with wood, iron and stone to save the fort. The forge was taken out of active use and disabled, for safety reasons, decades ago.

The building also housed the Trading Post operations for Old Fort Niagara, until the opening of the new Visitor Center in 2006, which included a new "Museum Shop" store. The Trading Post currently serves as a limited-stock satellite location for the primary shop, and all public food service on-site is located here.

Sketches by Clara Ritter, from 1934 Fort Niagara Guide.

Sketches by Clara Ritter, from 1934 Fort Niagara Guide.

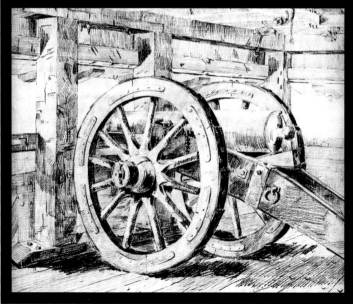

Segment from *Thundering Water*

Ne-ah-ga (Niagara Falls)

by Robert Griffing

From the Fort to the Falls: Historic Sites Relating to Old Fort Niagara

Although Fort Niagara is today only one small part of the modern Niagara Frontier community, it was the center of activity during the eighteenth century. The post's fortifications and buildings were symbols of the government which controlled the river. The military officer who commanded the fort held supreme power along the Niagara. His was the responsibility for keeping open the communication between Lakes Ontario and Erie, for maintaining good relations with the Native peoples, and for protecting the merchants who regularly traversed the Niagara Portage.

The carrying place around Niagara Falls provided the reason for maintaining a fort and garrison. Completion of the Erie Canal, in 1825, robbed Fort Niagara of its former strategic importance and shifted most development and commerce to the south end of the river. Thus, Buffalo became the metropolis of Western New York, while the Lower Niagara River remained largely rural.

In order to protect the portage and facilitate the movement of goods, Fort Niagara was supplemented by a number of small posts. Although these "dependencies" stretched the length of the portage, they were all administered as part of the post known as "Niagara." It is fortunate that many of these historic sites are located on public lands, often State or municipal parks. Access is generally unrestricted, except for US Coast Guard Station Niagara. Parking fees are charged seasonally at several sites, including Artpark and the Niagara Reservation State Park.

✪ THE BOTTOMS: The first point of interest may be viewed from several vantage points while touring Old Fort Niagara. The low land between the fort and the river is today occupied by a United States Coast Guard Station. The area was an important part of the eighteenth century post of Niagara. It offered easy access from the water to the top of the high river bank. This spot was the landing place for every vessel, whether canoe or sailing ship, which crossed Lake Ontario to Fort Niagara.

The French used this area as a landing, but did not build here. It was not until 1760 that much development took place. Following the British capture of Fort Niagara, merchants and traders from Albany and other cities of the American colonies flocked to the post. There they clamored for admittance to the Upper Great Lakes and access to the lucrative fur trade potential present to the west. Since hostile French and Indian forces still occupied Detroit and the other lake posts, the traders were detained at Niagara. In order to protect their goods, Fort Niagara's commanding officer constructed a number of warehouses on the low ground beneath the walls of the fort. Thus was founded the commercial center of Fort Niagara.

The civilian section was known by many names: "lower town," "trader town," and most commonly, "The Bottoms." From 1760 until the early 1790's, this was a rollicking, boisterous area of traders' stores, warehouses and grog shops. Though sometimes a nuisance to the army, the activities of the traders in The Bottoms could at least be carefully watched by the King's officers.

The British garrison also made use of The Bottoms. Although outside the main fortifications, the area was still sheltered by the walls. It was therefore a secure place to locate a number of facilities necessary for maintaining the troops. The wharf, firewood yard, boathouses, the Indian council house, and even private homes for some of the officers were located here. During the American Revolution, the Indian Department constructed many new buildings in The Bottoms to support their dealings with the Six Nations of the Iroquois.

The Bottoms lost much of its importance following American occupation in 1796. By that time, the British traders had transferred their operations to the Canadian side of the river. The remaining buildings were destroyed during the War of 1812. For most of the nineteenth century, The Bottoms were used primarily for the soldiers' gardens.

In 1893, the United States Life Saving Service established a station on the site. A hearty crew, equipped with oar propelled surf boats, stood ready to rescue imperiled Lake Ontario mariners. This was the direct consequence of a tragedy which took place some 22 years earlier on May 4, 1871, when eight members of the Fort Niagara Garrison (2 officers and 6 enlisted, all from Battery L, 1st US Artillery) drowned in Lake Ontario while attempting to retrieve a government issued lifesaving boat assigned to the post, which broke loose from its mooring during a severe storm. Officials in Washington realized and agreed quickly on the need for properly trained nautical professionals at the

Old Fort Niagara Archives.

US Life Saving Service launches boat at Fort Niagara, c. 1900.

site, but it took over twenty years to actually establish such a post! The Life Saving Service became part of the United States Coast Guard in 1915. Station Niagara, however, continued to be a busy place. During Prohibition years (1919-1933), an armed cutter was berthed here to intercept "rumrunners" attempting to cross from Canada. Today, the Coast Guard crew at Station Niagara is the last vestige of three hundred years of military occupation at the mouth of the Niagara River. Search and rescue are their principal missions, along with homeland security duties, and the interception of nautical drug-running and other smuggling operations. The Station House is the original 1893 Life Saving Service barracks/boathouse, with modifications and re-modeling over the years, the last being in 1998. The upper dormers of the Station House were designed, intentionally, to mimic the look of the French Castle in the old fort. A dedicated boat house, and a metal signal/beacon tower round out the station. The large on-site anchor was recovered from the river by Thor Borresen during the restoration of Old Fort Niagara, and was described at the time to be of French origin.

PLEASE NOTE: *Station Niagara is an active-duty United States Coast Guard facility. Permission should be obtained from the Station House before entering the grounds for official business.*

The 1871 Fort Niagara Lighthouse, c. 2007, as viewed from Niagara-on-the-Lake, Ontario, across the Niagara River, at the mouth of Lake Ontario.

Photo by Lawrence Fortunato. Used by permission.

The Fort Niagara Light, early 1900's.

Old Fort Niagara Archives. Official US Coast Guard Archive release.

✪ **THE FORT NIAGARA LIGHT (1871):** On the river side of the Old Fort Niagara parking lot is a lovely stone lighthouse. This building is the successor to the two early navigational beacons which stood on the French Castle. Its forty-five foot stone tower was constructed in 1871, and placed in service the following year. The light was elevated eleven feet in 1900 by the addition of a yellow brick extension. This provided a watchroom for the keeper. The keeper's house (now a private residence owned by NY State) and an iron building for the storage of lamp oil stand nearby. The Light (its operation later electrified and automated) cast a beam visible for fifteen miles using the original Fresnel lens, and was maintained by the Coast Guard until 1993, when it was decommissioned and replaced by a new high-power strobe-beacon system mounted on a steel mast next to the station house. The historic structure was ceded some five years later to the State of New York, but the Fresnel lens (removed and archived in 1995) remains the property of the Coast Guard.

The ground floor of the Fort Niagara Light is open, seasonally, to the public.

✪ **FORT NIAGARA MILITARY RESERVE:** The 284 acres surrounding Old Fort Niagara today comprise Fort Niagara State Park. This land was part of the military post for more than two hundred years. In 1760, less than one year after they had captured the fort from the French, the British carefully surveyed and laid out a military reserve. Their purpose was to prevent civilian encroachment on the fortifications. The original 716 acre military reserve included the modern State Park and part of the village of Youngstown.

During the eighteenth century, much of the military reserve was carefully cleared of trees and shrubs. This was, in part, due to the garrison's insatiable need for firewood, but there was a more important reason as well. Good defense required a clear field of fire of at least three hundred yards around the walls. This would prevent enemies from approaching unobserved, and expose them to fire from the fort.

The military utilized the reserve land for many other purposes. Garrison gardens were situated near the lake. A cemetery was located on the river side several hundred yards beyond the walls. Pastures were fenced and maintained for the garrison's cattle and sheep. The open space was used for occasional military executions and even soldiers' games. On these grounds in 1761 and 1764, Sir William Johnson, British Superintendant of Indian Affairs, held peace conferences with hundreds of Great Lakes Indians.

The Americans maintained the garrison reserve after their arrival in 1796. They resurveyed it in 1803, and reduced it to its present size in 1840. Then, shortly after the Civil War, a complex of unfortified barracks and officers' quarters, usually known as "New" Fort Niagara, was begun on the reserve lands. Hundreds of buildings were eventually constructed here between 1865 and 1945. The "New" Fort even held a camp for German prisoners of war between 1944 and 1946. The United States Army finally deactivated the post in 1963.

Several features of the Military Reserve are visible from the Old Fort Niagara parking lot. Across the parking lot from the Lighthouse are the remnants of the post motor pool. During the nineteenth century, animal stables had been located there. Several of the remaining buildings were erected prior to 1900, most prominently the red brick "Building 42" located at the entrance to the parking lot. It was constructed in 1897 as a warehouse for animal feed, but now houses the fort's Archaeology and Collections Care Center, including the Scott Archaeology Laboratory, which was named in honor of Dr. Stuart D. Scott and his wife, Patricia Kay Scott, who originated and nurtured the modern-era scientific archaeology program at Fort Niagara for nearly fifteen years, beginning in 1979.

The large red brick building immediately to the north of "Building 42" was known as "Building 102," but now serves as the Fort Niagara Visitor Center (converted in 2006), and includes museum exhibit galleries, and orientation theater, The Museum Shop and public restroom facilities. The structure was originally completed in 1939, and has served as a warehouse, Commissary, community school, and a variety of other uses over the years.

At the end of the parking lot opposite Old Fort Niagara, heavily shaded in trees, is the Post Cemetery. Though today popularly known as the "1812 Cemetery," it was in use long before that time. French, British and American soldiers were buried there from about 1755 until the last interment in 1949, in the gated area. A more recent burial was authorized in 1997 by executive order of the New York State Governor, for US Marine Corps aviator Major Michael Joseph Browne, a former member of the Old Fort Niagara Guard in his younger days, and Niagara University graduate (1982), whose grave is just outside the north line of the fence. He and 1st Lt. Robert B. Shaw were killed in a helicopter crash in Texas while piloting a "just overhauled" Bell AH-1W Cobra back to their base on the East Coast, from a Bell Textron Helicopter facilty. Both men were assigned to Marine Light Attack Helicopter Squadron 167, Marine Aircraft Group 26, Marine Corps Air Station, New River, North Carolina. Major Browne managed to maneuver the cripled machine away from a heavily populated area and high school about ten miles outside of Dallas, thus saving countless lives. The location was chosen because underground data on that spot was already known, and it was determined to be archaeologically neutral.

The cemetery proper may contain as many as 350 burials, and it is known that in decades and centuries past, a number of graves from the colonial period were exposed by shore erosion, and the remains lost to the river. Most of the existing markers date to the 1800's.

Late in the nineteenth century, the United States Army established a new post cemetery on the east side of the military reserve. Fortunately, a complete record of burials at that site was preserved. The remains there, military and civilian (including those of four World War II German soldiers who died as POW's at Niagara), were removed in 1949 to Woodlawn National Cemetery (a.k.a. Elmira National Cemetery), Elmira, New York, and recommitted on May 2nd. All of the extant grave markers at Niagara were believed to have been destroyed (by federal order), however, this was not the case, as a

PART OF LAKE ONTARIO

PLAN OF FORT NIAGARA
with its ENVIRON
Explanation

A *The Fort*
B *The Dock & Harbour*
C *Two Lime Kilns*
D *The Brick Kiln*
E *The Burying Place*
E *The Approaches*
G *The First Battery*
H *The Second Battery*
I *The Third Battery*

T H E

R I V E R

Scale
100 Fathoms to an Inch
50   100   200

British siege works, in relation to Fort Niagara in 1759, are shown in this engraving by Mary Ann Rocque, which appeared in *Plans of Forts in North America...* **(London 1763).**

Old Fort Niagara Archives.

number of them were sent to Elmira. New uniform markers, similar to those at Arlington National Cemeterty, were placed for the appropriate US military graves. It should be noted that according to an archived transcription of all the original markers done prior to the move, two sets of remains may have been reinterred in existing family plots elsewhere.

On the north (lake) side of the park, marked by the State Park swimming pools, is the site of the approaches constructed by the British during the 1759 siege of Fort Niagara. In order to overcome the defenses, the attackers literally dug their way toward the fort over a two week period. Batteries for heavy artillery were placed at intervals along the trench. From them, siege guns slowly pounded Fort Niagara into submission. The main part of the British lines stretched for some six hundred yards along the lake, from the east boundary of the park to the fort.

The British troops who laid siege to Fort Niagara had come from Oswego, about 150 miles to the east. Traveling in open boats, 2000 British soldiers and 1500 Iroquois warriors reached Niagara by coasting along the south shore of Lake Ontario. On July 6, they landed four miles east of Fort Niagara at "Le Petit Marais," a spot known today as Four Mile Creek. The mouth of the creek offered shelter from storms as well as from the French warships which cruised the lake. Once troops, artillery and supplies had been landed, the British army marched the remaining distance to Fort Niagara.

The site of the British landing is today encompassed by Four Mile Creek State Campsite. The area is restricted to campers and their guests, however, and is not usually accessible to the general public.

On the west side of the park, south of the cemetery, you will see scattered survivors of the nineteenth and twentieth century military buildings of New Fort Niagara (in addition to the previously discussed Building 42 and Building 102). Nearly all such structures were demolished in 1965-1966 during development of Fort Niagara State Park. The remaining brick buildings include the Officers' Club and Bachelor Officers' Quarters (1938), the Commandants House (1908), a large Federal Revival style barracks building (1938), and the Post Theater.

On the long stretch of road leading to the South or Youngstown Entrance to the park, you will see an extensive open area now filled with soccer fields. This was the site of a 1000 yard rifle range installed in 1885. The target butts were located near the lake. At the end of the soccer fields nearest the village of Youngstown, is the site of the World War II prisoner of war camp. From 1944 to 1946, temporary wooden buildings, surrounded by barbed wire and guard towers, held 1200 captured German soldiers. Many of these men had been part of General Erwin Rommel's famous Afrika Korps.

✪ **THE SALT BATTERY AND YOUNGSTOWN:** Two blocks beyond the South Entrance of Fort Niagara State Park, heading into Youngstown, is Salt Battery Park, identified by an historical marker. The park provides access to the edge of the bluff overlooking the Niagara River. Here, in the Fall of 1812, United States soldiers erected a battery from which heavy guns could bear on Fort George across the river. The fortification was known as the Salt Battery because salt barrels were used to build up its walls. Two more batteries were established along the river on each side of the Salt Battery. On May 25-26, 1813, guns at this site were instrumental in destroying Fort George. The range was so short for the heavy guns, that one American officer reported that he could see the wooden siding fly off the blockhouses of the British fort whenever one of his shots found its mark. The bombardment prepared the way for a successful amphibious landing at the mouth of the river on May 27. The American flag was raised over Fort George later that day.

Several historic sites are visible from Salt Battery Park. One mile to the north, at the mouth of the river, is Fort Niagara. Directly across the river, distant about six hundred yards, is Fort George, today preserved and maintained as a National Historic Site by Parks Canada. On the river bank below Fort George is copper-roofed Navy Hall, also a property of Parks Canada.

Navy Hall was an important part of the Fort Niagara complex during the eighteenth century, even though it lay on the other side of the river. The original building and wharf were constructed in 1765 to provide a base for the small British sailing vessels on Lake Ontario. The ships were laid up at the wharf for the winter, and the building served as a naval storehouse and barracks for the sailors. During the American Revolution, the riverbank downstream from Navy Hall and directly opposite Fort Niagara was occupied by barracks for Butler's Rangers, a regiment of Americans loyal to King George III, which saw much action on the frontier. At the conclusion of the American Revolution, refugee Loyalists, many of them discharged soldiers of Butler's Rangers, were settled on the lands opposite Fort Niagara. There they formed the beginnings of the modern community of Niagara-on-the-Lake and the nucleus of the Province of Ontario.

When United States troops occupied Fort Niagara in 1796, the British soldiers re-established themselves on the opposite side of the river. Expanding and incorporating the old Navy Hall complex, they had completed a new fort by 1799. Christened "Fort George" in honor of the reigning monarch (George III), the post changed hands and was burned twice during the War of 1812. The fortifications were finally abandoned in the mid-1820's. Fort George was reconstructed between 1937 and 1940. The original Navy Hall was also destroyed during the War of 1812. The current building is a replacement constructed in 1817 and restored during the reconstruction of Fort George.

Salt Battery Park is located in the village of Youngstown, one of the oldest communities on the New York side of the Niagara River. The settlement was established in the first decade of the nineteenth century by John Young, who located it just outside the boundary of the Fort Niagara Military Reserve. By the War of 1812, the settlement included about a dozen houses.

The war seriously disrupted civilian life along both sides of the Niagara. Youngstown's worst moment occurred late in 1813. On

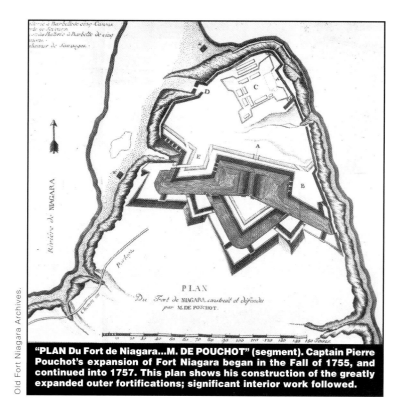

"PLAN Du Fort de Niagara...M. DE POUCHOT" (segment). Captain Pierre Pouchot's expansion of Fort Niagara began in the Fall of 1755, and continued into 1757. This plan shows his construction of the greatly expanded outer fortifications; significant interior work followed.

December 19, British troops silently marched through the village on their way to assault Fort Niagara. They quickly overcame the American advance guards who had taken shelter in the houses to escape the winter cold. After capturing the fort, the British burned the town.

Youngstown was rebuilt after the war, and was a prosperous community, port and shipbuilding center during the early nineteenth century. However, diversion of traffic by the Erie Canal (after 1825) ended hopes for a busy commercial port. Today, the village contains many fine examples of early nineteenth century residential architecture.

✪ **THE BATTLE OF LA BELLE FAMILLE (1759).** The Youngstown area also figured prominently in the French and Indian War. On July 24, 1759, near the end of the siege of Fort Niagara, a force of about 1500 French and allied Indians marched down the river from Niagara Falls, hoping to drive off the besiegers and relieve the gar-

rison. These troops had been gathered from French frontier posts as far west as Detroit, and were led by officers experienced in forest warfare. The British had been warned of their approach, however. On July 23, Sir William Johnson, the British commander, posted a detachment at a place on the road from the Falls known as "La Belle Famille." The redcoats were reinforced early the next morning as soon as the French force was sighted.

The French advanced confidently, believing themselves strong enough to defeat the British and fight their way through to Fort

Sketch by Clara Ritter (1934). OFN Archives.

Niagara. They were not ambushed, as some historians have reported, although they did indeed march into a well conceived lethal trap which had been set for them. In the words of one British officer, the French charged forward "with a very great noise and shouting," firing their muskets as they advanced. The 450 British soldiers coolly stood their ground until the French were only thirty yards away. When finally given the order to fire, the redcoats methodically delivered volleys of musket fire into the enemy ranks. In less than twenty minutes the French lines were shattered. The survivors, pursued by the British and their Iroquois allies, fled toward the Falls. The chase continued as far as the Niagara Escarpment at modern Lewiston, five miles up the river. French casualties were enormous, perhaps as many as 500 killed and captured. Defeat at the Battle of La Belle Famille ended French hopes that the defense of Fort Niagara could be successfully prolonged. On July 25, the day following the battle, the exhausted garrison capitulated.

Although several different locations have been claimed as the site of the Battle of La Belle Famille, the main action almost certainly occurred about one block south of Salt Battery Park at the modern junction of New York Routes 18F and 93. The intersection is marked by a traffic light in the very center of the village. An historical marker located about one mile south of the light, on New York 18F, is placed incorrectly to mark the main battle.

Near the south end of the village of Youngstown, along NY 18F, the road dips into a gully. On the west side of the road is an historical marker identifying the approximate location of the Fox Point Battery, last in the chain of six fortifications constructed by United States troops during the War of 1812 to bombard Fort George. A short distance further, on the east side, is another marker identifying the Battle of La Belle Famille. As previously noted, the actual site of that bloody clash was probably a mile to the north.

✪ **THE RIVER ROAD:** In traveling between Youngstown and Lewiston, on New York 18F, you drive over the earliest road in Western New York. The modern highway closely follows the route from Fort Niagara to the Falls, cut by French soldiers during the first half of the eighteenth century. Although boats could navigate the river as far as the site of Lewiston, the road was maintained to provide adequate land transportation. The River Road was in use by the 1740's.

Down this track in 1759, the unfortunate French relief column marched to defeat at La Belle Famille and later fled back toward the Falls. On December 19, 1813, a British assault party was more successful when they too, followed the River Road to capture Fort Niagara.

The steep banks of the Niagara River always presented a formidable obstacle to attempts to get ashore. The few gullies or other natural low spots in the banks provided rare and valuable landing places. One such site was a place known as Five Mile Meadows, so called because of its distance from the mouth of the river. "The Meadows," marked by the imposing red-roofed stone building of the Stella Niagara Education Park, sits between the road and the river. This natural landing was occupied by United States troops early in the War of 1812. They established a yard for building boats which were employed in the Spring of 1813 to convey troops across the river for the attack on Fort George. The garrison of Five Mile Meadows had been withdrawn long before the night of December 18-19, 1813, when British troops landed here to commence their march to Fort Niagara. The following day, the redcoats again passed up the River Road on their way to destroy the village of Lewiston.

✪ **THE LOWER LANDING:** Nestled in the south-west corner of the Village of Lewiston, along the Niagara River, is the New York State Earl W. Brydges Artpark. Within the boundaries of Artpark are several of the most significant early historic sites in Western New York. During the seventeenth and eighteenth centuries, this spot located at the foot of the Niagara Escarpment and the beginning of the Niagara River Gorge, was the natural northern terminus of the portage around the great Falls. The river was navigable to this point from Lake Ontario.

A short distance further south, however, the rapids and awesome cliffs of the gorge made further progress by water impossible.

The portage around Niagara Falls was by no means easy. The most arduous part, however, was the climb from the river to the top of the bank and thence to the summit of the escarpment. From there the road to the Upper Landing above the Falls crossed flat terrain. The "Lower" or downstream landing was, therefore, the most important single point along the portage.

The Lower Landing site was first used by the Native peoples who relied upon the lakes and rivers for travel. The earliest Europeans arrived late in 1678 as part of the expedition led by the explorer La Salle. They constructed some temporary cabins at the head of a gully which provided the only access from the river to the top of the bank. This ravine, on the east side of the river, was thereafter the principal landing spot for French and Indian travelers for the balance of the seventeenth century.

More permanent use of the Lower Landing commenced in 1720 when Louis-Thomas Chabert de Joncaire, a French trader and agent, obtained permission from the Seneca Indians to construct a trading post. He chose a location at the foot of the escarpment to establish his "Magazin Royale." Chabert's fortified house would be the only French post on the Niagara for the next six years. In 1726, the Magazin Royale was replaced by the stone building (the "French Castle") at Fort Niagara. The post at the Lower Landing was maintained, however, because the French found it convenient to have a storehouse at the north end of the portage. The last of these structures was burned by the Iroquois in 1759, during the siege of Fort Niagara.

The British also realized the importance of the Lower Landing. They re-established a small post on the site, in 1762, to provide a place to transfer goods up the cliff. This post became known commonly as "Fort Demler," after the lieutenant who directed its construction. During the Pontiac Uprising of 1763, the fort at the Lower Landing increased in importance, and was even attacked by hostile Indians in November of that year.

In the Spring of 1764, as part of the general fortification of the Niagara Portage, the British further strengthened the Lower Landing. The most notable improvement, however, was construction of a machine to move supplies up the hill. Actually, the device was a series of inclined planes, known as "The Cradles." Somewhat similar to the sliding carriages in a boathouse, these machines were powered by a

windlass, and could efficiently move boats and cargoe to the top of the escarpment. The Cradles operated in three stages. The first ran up the gully from the river to the top of the bank. After a turn of ninety degrees, the second segment paralleled the river to a natural shelf about halfway up the hill. The third stage completed the climb and terminated on the brow of the escarpment at a small stockaded fort, prosaically dubbed the "Principal Entrenchment on Mount Pleasant."

The garrison of Fort Demler was withdrawn in 1766, and the stockade and buildings accidentally burned the following year. The British, however, maintained various storehouses for goods until about 1790. At that point, with surrender of the New York shore to the United States imminent, they established a new landing site across the river at Queenston. The Cradles remained in operation for most of this time, though the upper two sections went out of use in 1765 because of the labor needed to power the windlass. The machine in the gully was employed to move goods to the top of the riverbank, where they were loaded into ox carts for the climb up the escarpment and the trip along the Portage Road to Niagara Falls.

The old landing site in the gully was used briefly by the Americans after 1796, but was soon replaced by a new wharf at Lewiston, about one half mile down the river. The surrounding area saw much military action during the War of 1812, with extensive camps for New York Militia established in the area during the first summer of the war. The disastrous October 13, 1812, attack on Queenston Heights commenced from the Lewiston shore.

From the main lower parking lot at Artpark, walk along the top of the riverbank toward the theater. Between the theater and the bank is the gully which gave the site its importance. Although this feature has been altered by erosion and construction, including a railroad trestle, it provides an idea of the steep climb from the river to the top of the bank. During the eighteenth century, a wharf was maintained at the base of the gully. The first stage of The Cradles ran up the ravine and terminated at the top of the slope. The machine then turned ninety degrees for the second stage of its ascent of the escarpment.

The north or downstream side of the gully was the site of Fort Demler and, later, a number of unfortified storehouses utilized by the British Army and traders. There was even a tavern for thirsty travelers here in the 1780's. This was the center of activity at the Lower Landing during the British period. From 1775 until 1790, a guard of less than a dozen men lived at the post. They were supplemented by larger detachments when provisions were to be moved across the portage.

From the head of the gully, moving east and then proceeding south up the road, one can look down on another parking lot situated beside the theater. Beneath the pavement lie the remains of Chabert de Joncaire's 1720 Magazin Royale. As originally constructed, this was a simple log house surrounded by a stockade. It stood near the head of the gully, conveniently situated for trade with Indians using the portage. Excavations at this spot in 1959-1960 uncovered evidence of the early eighteenth century French post.

Continuing up the hill, you reach the ground level above the modern theater, where the second stage of The Cradles terminated. From this point, there is an unobstructed view of the final upward thrust of the Niagara Escarpment. This was the route of the third stage of The Cradles. Although much of the hillside has been altered by construction of highways and Artpark, the section nearest the river gives some idea of the hill's appearance two hundred years ago.

From this point, it is possible to continue straight ahead through an old railroad cut and along a broad trail leading into the Niagara Gorge. Twelve thousand years ago this was the location of Niagara Falls. The constant erosion of rushing water has caused the Falls to recede to their present location six miles to the south. Here, one may easily appreciate the terrible obstacle presented to eighteenth century travelers by the gorge and the Falls.

Retracing your steps down the road, heading north, you will pass a path on your right, at the foot of the hill. About one hundred feet up the path is a prehistoric Indian burial mound. It is associated with the Hopewellian people of the Middle Woodland culture, who utilized the Niagara Portage some 1800 years ago.

As for Lewiston, it was another of the early settlements on the American side of the Niagara River. The village was strategically located at the terminus of the Ridge Road, the main highway west from Rochester in the first years of the nineteenth century. By the year 1800, settlers had moved into the western part of New York along this route, and had constructed houses at the site of Lewiston. By the War of 1812, the village was a thriving community with close ties to Canada.

Like other towns on both sides of the Niagara River, Lewiston fared badly during the war. Its location astride a key east-west road made it the destination for units of New York Militia called into service in the summer of 1812. A large military camp was established at Lewiston.

The troops spent the summer idle, however, while a truce prevented military action along the Niagara. The truce expired in October. On the 13th, American forces, by now composed of both regulars and militia, began crossing the river to invade Canada. At this critical moment, most of the New York Militia refused to leave the boundaries of the United States. Although the regular soldiers who crossed met with initial success in the Battle of Queenston Heights, they were eventually overwhelmed by a British counterattack. This stinging defeat of United States forces effectively ended the campaign of 1812 on the Niagara Frontier. Much of the battle site is today preserved by Parks Canada, and the Niagara Parks Commission. Queenston Heights, marked by the tall column of the Sir Isaac Brock Monument, is clearly visible across the river from Lewiston.

American successes in 1813 carried the war away from the village. On December 19, however, following the capture of Fort Niagara, British soldiers and their Indian allies appeared on the road from Youngstown. They quickly brushed aside resistance from a small body of American troops and systematically burned the village. It was rebuilt after the war. Much of the architecture visible today is typical of Western New York in the first half of the nineteenth century.

✪ **THE PORTAGE ROAD:** The actual track of the Portage Road, moving south from the Niagara Escarpment above Lewiston, is today under Route 104. While the portage was in operation, ox carts hauled goods and boats up this hill on their way to the Upper Landing above Niagara Falls.

At the brow of the escarpment was the site of "The Principal Entrenchment on Mount Pleasant," a fortification constructed by British Engineer Lieutenant John Montresor in 1764. It guarded the terminus of The Cradles which began their long climb at the Lower Landing below. The stockade and storehouses there were maintained for only one year. The site was later reused by the Americans in 1812 for construction of Fort Grey, a battery placed to bear on British positions in Queenston. It played an active part in the Battle of Queenston Heights.

Once at the top of the Niagara Escarpment, the Portage Road traversed flat, forested terrain for six miles. The land was cut by many small creeks flowing into the gorge. These were bridged by soldiers from Fort Niagara who also repaired the road as needed. The Portage Road followed the river to Devil's Hole, where it cut away from the

Native peoples from numerous Indian nations traveled to or through Niagara for trade, Indian conferences at the Fort, and as military allies of France, Britain and the United States. Old Fort Niagara received its National Historic Landmark designation, in large part, because it was a significant cross-cultural contact point between Europeans and Native Americans, including many tribes of the Mid-West and West of North America. Archaeological evidence confirms use of the Fort Niagara site by ancient peoples going back some 10,000 years, following the end of the Ice Age and recession of the great inland lake which cover this part of the continent. *Above: Native warrior of the French & Indian War period.*

gorge to head toward the Upper Landing. To trace the actual portage route as it exists today, one should taking Route 104 South (Lewiston Road) from Lewiston, up the Niagara Escarpment and into the city of Niagara Falls. There, Route 104 becomes Main Street. At the Niagara Falls Public Library, the original portage bears to the left away from Main Street (Route 104), and follows modern Portage Road to the Upper Niagara River at Buffalo Avenue. The area is today heavily ur-banized.

During the summer of 1764, Lieutenant Montresor erected a series of small picketed posts, termed "redoubts," along the length of the Portage Road. Nine little forts were spaced at intervals of six hundred to one thousand yards. They sheltered guard detachments to protect the Portage Road and its users from a repetition of the ambush at Devil's Hole, which will be discussed next. The portage redoubts were abandoned as soon as the Indian Uprising of 1763-1764 had been subdued.

✪ **DEVIL'S HOLE:** Along the Niagara River Gorge, immediately south of the massive Robert Moses Niagara Power Plant (New York State Power Authority), and Niagara University, is Devil's Hole State Park. Although primarily a point of geological and scenic interest, it was also the site of the worst defeat of British forces during the great Indian Uprising of 1763-1764.

When the Native tribes of the Great Lakes rose against the British, in the Spring of 1763, they quickly captured every small military post west of Niagara, with the single exception of Detroit. Since Detroit was always supplied through Niagara, the desperate plight of its iso-lated garrison further increased the importance of the portage.

Throughout the summer of 1763, supplies and reinforcements for the beleaguered garrison flowed across the carrying place. The road was poorly protected, however, and far from the main garrison at Fort Niagara. Exposed as it was, the Portage Road was sure to be attacked. The blow fell on September 14, as a number of lightly escorted wag-ons were returning to the Lower Landing for another load of provi-sions. A large number of hostile Seneca Indians lay in wait along the road. As the wagons approached the creek flowing into Devil's Hole, they rumbled across a small wooden span later known as "Bloody Bridge." It was here the Senecas sprung their trap. John Stedman, a civilian employee of the army, was able to spur his horse out of danger and escape to Fort Schlosser at the Upper Landing. The rest of the teamsters and guards perished. The Senecas, well aware of the importance of interrupting the movement of provisions, systematically destroyed the draft animals and threw harness and wagons into the gorge. It was weeks before the British could again transport supplies to Detroit in the necessary quantities.

British misfortunes were not yet over, however. Gunfire from the ambush was heard at the Lower Landing two miles down the river. Two companies of troops led by Lieutenant George Campbell were encamped there on their way to Detroit. Hearing the firing, Campbell ordered his men forward at the double...directly into a second ambush! Eighty British soldiers died slightly north of Devil's Hole in "Campbell's Defeat," the worst of the war. Only eight wounded men eventually made their way back to Fort Niagara.

One of the most intriguing stories of this incident concerns a reputed survivor, Drummer Lemuel Matthews of the 80th Regiment of Foot. Trapped in the second ambush, Matthews either jumped or was thrown into the three hundred foot deep Niagara Gorge. The horrifying fall was broken when his leather drum sling snagged a tree limb! Matthews escaped and later lived out his days near Queenston, only a short distance from the site of his miraculous escape. Though the story might be apocryphal, it was current as early as 1812, nine years before Matthews' death.

Devil's Hole Park provides a good view of the Lower Rapids of the Niagara River. A short distance downstream from the parking lot is the Devil's Hole itself. This natural feature, created by the erosion of a small stream, was a well known landmark on the eighteenth century portage. A trail leads down the Devil's Hole to the riverbank, and then continues one mile upstream to a flight of steps leading out of the gorge at Whirlpool State Park. Additionally, a walking trail follows the rim of the gorge for one mile upstream to Whirlpool State Park.

The Portage Road swung away from the river at this point, marked by present day Route 104. The low ridge above the highway was the site of Redoubt Number 3, built in 1764.

✪ **THE FALLS OF NIAGARA:** The runoff of the four upper Great Lakes is constricted into the Niagara River and drops 182 feet over the great cataracts of Niagara. The Falls were, needless to say, objects of wonder to the earliest European explorers. Their documented discovery occurred late in 1678 when Father Louis Hennepin and other members of La Salle's expedition viewed them from the American side.

"Cataracte de Niagara, Tom XIV, No. IX" Engraving by Pierre Quentin Chedel (after Fr. Louis Hennepin), in "Histoire Generales," by Abbe Antoine Francois Prevost, Paris: Chez Didot, 1757.

Old Fort Niagara Archives.

Descriptions of Niagara Falls soon appeared in European publications. The natural wonder aroused much curiosity. As travel to the interior became more practical in the eighteenth century, a few affluent and hardy Europeans and Americans began to visit solely for the purpose of seeing the Falls of Niagara. These travelers were warmly received by the officers of Fort Niagara who were starved for "genteel" company. Most visitors in the last half of the eighteenth century could expect an escort of an officer or two for the ride up the Portage Road to the Falls. Overnight accommodations were provided by John Stedman who regaled the curious with tales of his escape from the Devil's Hole ambush. The cataracts were the chief attraction, however. Since the view of the Horseshoe (Canadian) Falls was limited from the east bank, many of the more adventuresome descended rickety ladders to the bottom of the gorge. Others could find experienced boatmen to row them to the upper end of Goat Island...and back! Few were disappointed by the experience.

The great Falls were a constant part of life at eighteenth century Fort Niagara. According to all accounts, the roar of falling water could

"*Moment in Time*"
by
Kathleen Giles

be heard at Fort Niagara, nearly thirteen miles away. The towering plume of mist hanging above the cataracts was visible from the fort, and was even used as a landmark by sailors on Lake Ontario.

The mainland opposite the upper end of Goat Island was the site of the first industrial use of the awesome power of Niagara Falls. It is possible that the Frenchman Daniel Chabert de Joncaire operated a sawmill there in the 1750's. The first well documented mill was erected during the British occupation, however. In 1768, Francis Pfister, post engineer at Fort Niagara but also a private entrepreneur and co-concessionaire of the Niagara Portage operation, built a mill to saw planks. It was in use for about a decade, until replaced in the 1780's by mills on the Canadian side.

The modern city of Niagara Falls, New York, had its origins in the village of Manchester, established about 1805 and named for the mill town of Manchester, England. The new village was sited to exploit the water power of the Falls.

Approximately two miles to the east of downtown Niagara Falls, along the upper Niagara River, sit the New York Power Authority Water Intakes. From this point, most of the early historic sites of the upper river may be seen.

✪ **THE UPPER LANDING:** The head of the Niagara Portage was situated at a point where the river's current was slack enough to allow small boats to safely re-enter the water and proceed to Lake Erie. This occurs about one mile above the Falls. This location was probably the place used by prehistoric travelers and the early European explorers and traders.

It was some years after their arrival before the French felt a need for a formal post at the head of the portage, or the "Upper Landing" as it was commonly known. The permanent post established at Fort Niagara in 1726 had gained them effective control of the route to the West, and barred the British from further penetration of the Great Lakes. It was not so easy to control movement of the Indians. For tribesmen of the Great Lakes, the lure of inexpensive British trade goods was considerable. By crossing the portage and slipping past the fort at the mouth of the river, Native traders could proceed to the British post at Oswego on the southeastern end of Lake Ontario. The French eventually moved to protect their trade monopoly. In 1751 they built a small picketed fort and storehouse at the head of the portage. Named "Little Niagara," this post was commanded by Ensign Daniel Chabert de Joncaire, son of the man responsible for establishing a French presence on the Niagara at the Lower Landing in 1720 and at Fort Niagara in 1726. The new fort was effective, and did much to keep the fur trade in French hands. Fort Little Niagara was also useful for supporting the French military expeditions which crossed the Niagara Portage in the early 1750's, on their way to establish posts in the Ohio Valley. The end came for Fort Little Niagara in 1759. When the British appeared before Fort Niagara the small garrison was recalled to the main post to aid in its defense. As they abandoned the tiny stockade on July 8, the French soldiers set walls and buildings ablaze.

Although the British were quick to use the Upper Landing, a year passed before they reconstructed the fort. In 1760, the need for a guard at the head of the portage resulted in erection of a new stockade somewhat farther up the river. At first, the British also called their post Fort Little Niagara. Following a further rebuilding in 1763, however, the place was renamed Fort Schlosser in honor of the officer who had directed the work.

Within a few years, the Upper Landing had become the center of portaging activities and the headquarters of Francis Pfister and John Stedman. These men, the former a military officer and the latter a civilian, had by 1766 obtained the concession to operate the carrying place. Their lucrative business as "masters of the portage" included moving goods for private traders and the British government. They maintained barns, storehouses and a residence at the Upper Landing, as well as storehouses and The Cradles at the Lower Landing. After 1773, Stedman operated the portage alone. He later passed on the business to his brother Philip, and then his nephew, Philip, Jr. The Stedmans' little transportation empire lasted until 1790, when the portage route was moved to the west side of the Niagara River.

The military occupation of Fort Schlosser was somewhat sporadic. Following regular use from 1761 to 1766, its garrison was withdrawn to Fort Niagara and the buildings turned over to Pfister and Stedman. The outbreak of the American Revolution required increased security on the portage, however, and the little post was reoccupied about 1775. It was rebuilt four years later. Fort Schlosser was occupied by a detachment of British soldiers until sometime between 1793 and 1796. Thereafter, the buildings deteriorated until the remaining few were destroyed during the War of 1812. The United States Army made little use of the post after their occupation of Niagara in 1796. Around 1805, a village known as "Schlosser" sprang up at the site. As the two hamlets of Manchester and Schlosser grew, they merged to form the village of Niagara Falls.

The main features of the Upper Landing and the Upper River are visible from the Power Authority Water Intake parking area. On the extreme right, as one faces the river, are Niagara Falls, marked by the beginning of the rapids and a column of mist. The French landing and the original Fort Little Niagara were located approximately one mile above the Falls at a point also to the right. Fort Schlosser was a mile nearer (also to the right). Its site is today occupied by an industrial area at the end of modern Portage Road.

Directly opposite is the west or Canadian shore. To the left, however, the Niagara River is split into two channels by Grand Island (New York). The east channel is marked by the Grand Island Bridges. The west channel between Grand Island and the Canadian shore is directly in front of you. The latter was the route followed by boats on their way up and down the river. The west channel is split by Navy Island (Canada), so called because of a shipyard established there in 1761. By 1764, the British had constructed five sailing vessels at Navy Island for service on Lake Erie. The shipyard was abandoned in the late 1760's in favor of Detroit.

The naval vessels constructed on Navy Island had to be laid up each winter while ice closed the Great Lakes. For a few years in the 1760's, the vessels were moored at Navy Island or in a small creek at the north western end of Grand Island. The entrance to the creek, which soon became the preferred spot, is visible just to the right of the end of the Grand Island Bridges. Those crossing the bridge on their way to Buffalo will see the swampy creek just past the toll plaza. In 1766, the ship *Victory* caught fire during winter lay-up and burned to the water line. Two years later, the *Boston* shared her fate. Thereafter, the spot was known as "Burnt Ship Creek." After 1769, all the Lake Erie naval vessels wintered at Detroit.

The final element of the portage system was Fort Erie, located on the shore of Lake Erie, sixteen miles further up the Niagara River. There, goods and supplies were loaded into sailing vessels for the journey to Detroit and Michilimackinac. Fort Erie was established in 1764 on the west side of the river (present day Fort Erie, Ontario, Canada). It thus remained in British territory after 1796. The fort figured prominently in the battles of the War of 1812, and was destroyed during that conflict. It was reconstructed in the 1930's, and is today operated as a historic site museum by the Niagara (Ontario) Parks Commission.

Daybreak, December 19th, 1813: a British assault force under the command of Colonel John Murray, captured Fort Niagara after a brief but vicious surprise attack. The entire garrison was captured or killed. The raiders consisted of elements from the 41st and 100th Regiments, the Royal Scots, the 52nd Battery of the Royal Artillery, and Canadian Mililtia. The detachment from the 52nd Battery was under the command of Lieutenant Charlton, and they were cited in official dispatches for gallantry that day, and later at the Battle of Lundy's Lane (where they were took massive casualties). The Battery was awarded the honor of having the designation "NIAGARA" added to their name...an honor which continues to this day. The *52nd (Niagara) Battery*, Royal Artillery, officially celebrates "Niagara Day" every December 19th, and their official crest includes an image of the French Castle at Fort Niagara.

Photos by Lawrence Fortunato. Used by permission.

The Capture of Fort Niagara by British Forces on December 19, 1813:
An Eyewitness Account by Robert Lee, Esq.

Writings on the aftermath of the capture of Fort Niagara by British forces in December of 1813, seldom speak of what happened to the prisoners taken. The published account of Robert Lee, a United States civilian who was there at the time, gives light to this neglected aspect of the story, and includes an account of degredations to female captives. Lee was a rather prominent citizen of the region who chaired the official meeting at which the first Supervisor of the Town of Cambria, NY, was selected, following the establishment of that entity by the Niagara County Legislature. Lee's narrative was published in the *Buffalo Gazette,* sometime following his release, and was reprinted in *THE WAR,* a weekly newspaper "published every Tuesday morning by S. Woodworth & Co., *No. 60 Vesey-St. near the Bear-Market, N. York,*" from which the following is transcribed (original issue in Fort Niagara Publications Archive). Considering that Buffalo was burned by the British some ten days after Fort Niagara fell, it is interesting to note that *The Buffalo Gazette* was up and running shortly after.

• • • • • • • • • • • • • •

THE WAR
NEW-YORK.....TUESDAY,
FEBRUARY 8, 1814   Vol. II. — No. 34.

From the Buffalo Gazette.
INTERESTING PARTICULARS OF THE FALL OF
FORT NIAGARA

"Robert Lee, esq.[,] late of Fort Niagara, has just returned from the province of Upper Canada, where he had been taken as a prisoner, on the surrender of Fort Niagara. Not having seen anything like a correct account of the loss of our fort — of the slaughter of our brave soldiers, or of the enemy's treatment to them and our fellow citizens they had taken prisoners; we feel a melancholy satisfaction in now having it in our power to give the particulars of that tragical event from a gentleman so intelligent and so well acquainted with the situation of Fort Niagara, and of the subsequent conduct of the enemy."

"The fort was attacked[,] or rather[,] entered by the enemy about 4 o'clock on the morning of the 19th ult. So silent was this done, that the garrison was not alarmed when the enemy entered the gates of the fort. On their entering, some firing took place between the guard at the southeast block house, and the sick in the red barracks, on the part of the Americans, and the enemy that had and were entering the gate. The whole American force in the fort at that time, was at least 400, including men of all descriptions. Three hundred and fifty of those were able and willing to defend the fort to the last extremity, in the way the impotent and convalescent were able to do, to wit, firing on the enemy from the block house, barracks, &c. The principal, and in fact the only resistance the enemy met with, was from the sick in the red barracks and the guard at the southeast block house. From the order of congratulation that was issued by the enemy the same morning, it appeared we had lost 65 in killed, and 15 wounded; the wounds, as the order said, were by the bayonet; but this order was issued very soon after they had got possession of the fort, and did not include 15 of our poor fellows that were afterwards bayonetted in the cellars of the houses. Our whole number killed was at least 80. The British force that took possession was about 400, commanded by col. Murray, who was wounded in the arm, in entering the gate — the command then devolved upon col. Hamilton. The private property in the fort was given up to plunder. He does not believe that any individual saved any thing, except the clothes he had on. Capt. Leonard, the American commander, was at his house about two miles distant from the fort, and hearing the attack, rode towards the fort and was made prisoner and kept in close confinement two days and a half; how much longer the informant does not know. A non-commissioned officer and about 20 privates made their escape about the time of the attack, by scaling the pickets. Our soldiers were kept two days in close and miserable confinement in the fort, without the use of provisions, and with a very scanty supply of wood and water, at the expiration of which, both the citizens and soldiers were crossed over the river and lodged in a part of what had been the British magazine, at Fort George, and in open plank and board huts; in either situation it was impossible to lay down. The magazine was so filthy that many of the prisoners became infested with vermin.

They remained there seven days; the citizens were then removed to a brick building near Queenston, where they were so much crowded that it was impossible to take any kind of comfort, either by day or night. The supply of provisions was not only scanty, but of the worst kind; meat of the most inferior and repulsive quality, and bread that cannot be described, both at this place and at the magazine &c. What water the prisoners used they had to purchase. The informant believes, that through the influence of a gentleman resident in Upper Canada, himself, together with ten other citizens, were permitted to cross to the United States. On the 13th inst. the residue of the citizens, to the amount of about 70, were marched under a strong guard to Burlington Heights, and from thence it was said and believed they would be sent to Kingston. It was a matter of frequent conversation and exultation between the British non-commissioned officers and the privates, while the informant was a prisoner under guard, that the Americans cried out and begged for quarters, but they bayonetted, or rather, in their language, skivered them, notwithstanding. The women and children that were taken at or near Lewiston, were stripped of the principal part of their clothing, shoes, &c.[,] and taken across the river. After the informant was permitted to cross, he applied for some kind of protection from the British commander from their parties of Indians and others, scouring on the American side of the river; but was answered he could have none — he and the rest must make the best of their way to the American line."

"POSTSCRIPT.

"We stop the press to say, that at an express arrived at Batavia, yesterday morning, and states that the British had been reinforced at Fort Niagara: that they had made sally from the fort and had burnt all the buildings to the Four Mile Creek, on the lake."

• The Rush-Bagot Treaty •

The naval force to be maintained upon the American Lakes by His Majesty and the Govermment of the United States shall henceforth be confined to the following vessels on each side, that is —

- *On Lake Ontario, to one vessel not exceeding one hundred tons burden, and armed with one eighteen pound cannon.*

- *On the upper lakes, to two vessels, not exceeding like burden each, and armed with like force.*

- *On the waters of Lake Champlain, to one vessel not exceeding like burden, and armed with like force.*

All other armed vessels on these lakes shall be forthwith dismantled, and no other vessels of war shall be there built or armed.

If either party should hereafter be desirous of annulling this stipulation, and should give notice to that effect to the other party it shall cease to be binding after the expiration of six months from the date of such notice.

The naval force so to be limited shall be restricted to such services as will, in no respect, interfere with the proper duties of the armed vessels of the other party.

• Archaeology at Fort Niagara •

The twelve acres of Old Fort Niagara and the adjacent United States Coast Guard Station comprise one of the most important archaeological sites in the Great Lakes region. The existing buildings and walls of the fort represent only a fraction of the construction which occurred over three hundred years on this historic point of land. Current research indicates that as many as 250 major buildings were erected within the boundaries of the site between the seventeenth century and the 1930's. Hundreds more stood in New Fort Niagara. Their remains lie beneath the grassy parade grounds and soccer fields.

The archaeological significance of this site has only been realized in more recent times. Though some digging was conducted in the late 1920's and early 1930's, the first scientific work began in 1979 under the direction of Dr. Stuart D. Scott, then of the State University of New York at Buffalo. Field seasons since that time have resulted in the identification of dozens of architectural features and the recovery of thousands of artifacts from the Native American, French, British, and American periods of occupation.

Archaeological research and the conservation and study of its results, are ongoing activities at Old Fort Niagara, and vary each year in scope and focus. Support from many quarters, public and private, and the efforts of numerous dedicated volunteers have permitted the complex process of uncovering the past to continue.

Photo, courtesy of Rory Bialecki. Used by permission.

• For Further Reading •

• Pierre Pouchot, *Memoirs on the Late War in North America Between France and England,* Revised Edition (Youngstown, New York, 2004). Translated from the original Yverdon Edition by Michael Cardy. Edited, with Notes, by Brian Leigh Dunnigan.

• Frank H. Severance, *An Old Frontier of France* (2 vols.; New York, 1917).

• Brian Leigh Dunnigan, *Siege, 1759: The Campaign Against Niagara,* Revised Edition (Youngstown, New York, 1996).

• Donale E. Graves (Ed.), Soldiers of 1814: *American Enlisted Men's Memoirs of the Niagara Campaign,* (Youngstown, New York, 1995).

• Robert Malcolmson (Ed.), *Sailors of 1812: Memoirs and Letters of Naval Officers on Lake Ontario,* (Youngstown, New York, 1997).

• Lois Huey and Bonnie Pulis, *Molly Brant: A Legacy of Her Own,* (Youngstown, New York, 1997).

• Roland L. Nafus, *Navy Island – Historic Treasure of the Niagara: Heritage, Archaeology, Folklore,* (Youngstown, New York, 1998).

• John C. Fredriksen, *Green Coats and Glory: United States Regiment of Riflemen, 1808-1821,* (Youngstown, New York, 2000).

• Lois Demler, *Pease Porridge: Beyond the King's Bread – Cooking at Niagara,* (Youngstown, New York, 2003).

• Louis L. Babcock, *The War of 1812 on the Niagara Frontier* (Buffalo, 1927).

• Lura Lincoln Cook, *The War of 1812 on the Frontier,* (Buffalo, 1961).

• E.A. Cruikshank, *Butler's Rangers,* (Welland, Ontario, 1893). Reprinted (Niagara Falls, Ontario, 1975).

• Stephen G. Strach, *The British Occupation of the Niagara Frontier* (Niagara Falls, Ontario, 1976).

• Howard Swigget, *War Out of Niagara* (New York, 1933).

• Barbara Graymont, The Iroquois in the American Revolution (Syracuse, 1972).

• David L. Dickson, "Four Grand Murals and the Artists of the Fort Niagara Officers" Club & Bachelor Officers Quarters," Old Fort Niagara Edition (Youngstown, New York, 2007).

Since 1927,
The mission of the
Old Fort Niagara Association has been the
preservation and restoration of
Old Fort Niagara.
A 501 (c) (3) Not-for-Profit
membership organization open to everyone,
the group operates the historic site
under license from the State of New York.

For more information on the work of the Association
and its year-round programs
(including *Living History* & *Distance Learning* opportunities)
please contact us at:
Old Fort Niagara Association
Fort Niagara State Park
P.O. Box 169
Youngstown, NY 14174-0169
Phone: (716)745-7611 • http://www.oldfortniagara.org

Photo by Lawrence Fortunato. Used by permission.